£5.00

WITHDRAWN
University of
Illinois Library
at Urbana-Champaign

John Dunton
TEAGUE LAND

John Dunton (1659-1733) loved books, ladies and politics. In 1698, separating from his wife and mother-in-law, he went to Ireland on a visit which was marked by the sort of rows and entanglements which became typical of his later life.

This book consist of letters by Dunton in the Rawlinson Manuscripts in the Bodleian Library. They describe: A Journey to Galway; Iar-Connacht; A Baptism, A Wake and a Funeral; Co. Kildare, a Wedding, Malahide and Drogheda; Dublin.

JOHN DUNTON

Teague Land, or
A Merry Ramble
to the
Wild Irish

LETTERS FROM IRELAND, 1698
EDITED BY EDWARD MACLYSAGHT

IRISH ACADEMIC PRESS

The content of this book was previously published as an appendix to Edward MacLysaght, *Irish Life in the 17th Century* (first edition Cork 1939).

© Edward MacLysaght 1982

ISBN 0 7165 0291 7

Printed in 1982 in the Republic of Ireland for Irish Academic Press Limited, Kill Lane, Blackrock, County Dublin.

Acknowledgement

The editor gratefully acknowledges the permission granted by the Bodleian Library, Oxford, to print the letters which make up this book

CONTENTS

Preface 7
1 A Journey to Galway 9
2 Iar-Connacht 17
3 A Baptism, a Wake and a Funeral 29
4 Co. Kildare; a Wedding 40
5 Malahide and Drogheda 51
6 Dublin 67

PREFACE

The following hitherto unpublished letters by John Dunton are taken from the Rawlinson Manuscripts in the Bodleian Library, Oxford, (Rawl. D. 71). Mr. Charles McNeill's report on these MSS. is printed in *Analecta Hibernica*, No. 3. Apparently the letters in question were intended for publication under the title of " Teague Land, or A Merry Ramble to the Wild Irish " ; Dunton certainly mentions several times in his " Conversation in Ireland " his intention of publishing an account of his further " rambles." It must be noted, however, that certain passages in these unpublished letters are used verbatim by him in his " Conversation," e.g., that relating to racing at the Curragh. Mr. McNeill refers to a collection of six letters, but I have reckoned in a seventh, the one describing the legal system and religious denominations in the country, as it evidently belongs properly to the series, though actually a considerable part of it was printed in his " Conversation " (*Dublin Scuffle*, 1699 edn. pp. 330 to 335, and *Life and Errors*, 1818 edn. pp. 554 to 559), and consequently I have not reprinted it here.

In deciding to omit certain passages from these letters I have been guided solely by the extent to which they are of value in giving us a picture of life in Ireland at the end of the seventeenth century: as long as he does this the author's coarseness has not prevented me from transcribing the original exactly as it was written ; but I think it would be making altogether too much of John Dunton to print the bawdy stories which he retells at second hand (with the salacious relish we might expect from that old hypocrite) when they throw little or no light on the everyday life of that period. Dunton can be boring as well as obscene, and I have omitted without hesitation his tedious descriptions of a christening and other rites since in these he is obviously relying not on his own memory, but on the words printed in some prayer-book which he consulted afterwards.

At the risk of inconsistency I have adhered to Dunton's own spelling in one letter (viz. No. 2) and modernized it in the others.

E. MacL.

Letter No. 1

Since Nature not without a long nine months cookery has fitted us to enter into the world, and the care of our parents or friends is generally employed for qualifying us to make some figure therein, I think them unworthy of both who, having made any considerable observations upon its stage, basely to confine them within their own breasts without affording their fellows the benefits or diversions which they may receive thereby. If then anything in my ramble be worth their notice it is from you they must receive it, as a debt wholly due to you both by my promise and inclination, and if the following account have anything useful or agreeable to you I am sure the rest of the world which sees it will not be disgusted at it, especially if they be blest with the same apprehensions that you are. To begin then.

Having first furnished my pockets with necessary cash, which you know will make the mare go, if the spurs be not blunt nor the switch broken, I got upon the outside of an easy pad nag, for you may observe that since the Trojan wooden horse none have been heard to travel in the inside of their palfrey, and following my nose which pointed westward, the first place I arrived at was Chapel Izod, a country house within two little miles of Dublin seated upon the banks of the Liffey, and by the wall of the Deer Park whereto the Governors of this kingdom commonly retire from the fatigues of their court. There is little remarkable here more than the situation, which lying between two heights upon a pleasant smooth river, makes it agreeable enough. In the summer at that time the Lady Marchioness of Winchester was lying in childbed here of the young Lord Nassau Pawlet.

From hence I jogged on through Palmers Town, St. Catherines, and Leixlip, all upon the banks of the river, and though they be not so fine as Windsor, Hampton Court or Kensington, yet I assure you they are seats not unworthy a private gentleman's residence, or a stranger's consideration, especially if he be prepossessed with so mean an opinion of the country as I was; the swans in the water, a number of fishermen, on the banks the boscage, and some wood made me regard it as very agreeable landscape, and perhaps you will wonder if three so good houses and pleasant seats did lately belong all to one private gentleman not dignified with any higher mark of quality than that of an esquire.

I made so much use of mine eyes in staring about that forgetting the use of my heels it was dinner time before my horse brought me to Maynooth, ten miles from Dublin. It is a tolerable village with one or two good inns where meat is well dressed, and good liquors to be had; here are the remains of a very stately castle belonging to the Earls of Kildare. In days of yore it was accounted so impregnable a place, that after the English got it into their hands an Act of Parliament was passed here against ever rebuilding it, and yet if it were now in the most fortified condition it was ever said to be, it could not resist one day our present methods of attack, so much is the art of destroying improved since the cursed invention of gunpowder. I cannot forbear acquainting you with a story related to me which perhaps will contradict the common received opinion of the Irish woman's chastity. . . .

[The story is not worth printing, though unlike most of Dunton's anecdotes this one reflects credit on the heroine of it.]

A little beyond this town is an heap of stones just by the highway laid there as a monument of the Lord of Taragh's death, who they say in that place fell from his horse upon a wound received from Sir F. B. I should not have taken notice of so inconsiderable a thing but that thereby I am led to acquaint you with [a] piece of Irish poetry inscribed upon that Lord's tombstone in St. James's churchyard in Dublin.

> The Generous and Illustrious Thomas Preston
> Lord Viscount of Taragh lyes under this stone
> In the Prime of his Youth about twenty and one
> This hopeful blossom was cropped and gone.

I went out that evening thirteen miles further to a place called Clonard, where I took up my lodging at the best inn in the town, and though this was the first public house that I lay in since my coming into this Country yet I found nothing here more than the misfortune of want so epidemical a thing in Ireland, else my landlord and his wife were English like enough in their behaviour; but my curiosity setting me upon inquiry after everything, that among them all I might cull something worth remembering, I was informed of one who could and did give an account of what kind of death hanging was, I am also the more emboldened to relate it because I have since had it confirmed by a person of known integrity who had it from the mouth of the man that was hanged, his name was Sadler and formerly kept an inn at Clonard ; he came into this country a soldier under Oliver Cromwell in whose troop I forget but a trooper he was, he with some others of the Army were surprised by a party of the Irish who led them all into an adjacent wood, and began to cut small hazel switches, he said, the English did suppose the enemy intended to whip them to death, for they understood not one word of Irish and the others spoke not one word of English, but after they had cut a sufficient number of hazels they fell to twisting them, which immediately informed the poor Oliverians that they were making gads instead of ropes to hang them. I never inquired what Sadler's thoughts upon this occasion [were] but believe they were the same that the surprising approach of the like destiny would have put into you or me. In short after stripping they were all trussed upon the trees and left to die and feed the crows, but it pleased God to bring another party of English that way who perhaps guessed what they were by the barbarity used to 'em, and cut them down. Sadler was the only man who discovered any signs of life, him they took care of and carried home to their quarters where the poor man recovered and lived long enough to be revenged upon some of the inhuman rogues ; the account he gave of himself was that in the first moment of his suspension he fancied a mighty flash of light before his eyes, and was insensible of everything after until he found himself in the arms of his friends, his neck was awry ever after his head inclining to the opposite side that the knot was placed on.

I am now in the County of Westmeath, a country at this time well inhabited by English though before the late Rebellion I am told the Irish had as landlords and tenants in their hands as much land of that county as came to £30,000 per annum, but now very few considerable parcels of land are occupied by them. The next stage I made was Mullingar, the shire town lying in a fair plain country without anything remarkable save only its Lough which indeed is a very large and fine being [*blank*] miles [and] over [*blank*] in length. It is plentifully stored with eel, roach and pike, some of these of so large a size as would stagger the belief of those in England for I am very well assured there has been taken of this fish six foot and a half long, which considering the bulk and firmness and excellency of it sauced would in London be a present worthy of the King.

Old stories in this country tell that where the Lough or lake now is a fair town once stood and people in a dry summer when cotting, that is rowing in a small sort of boat, have discovered the tops of many houses and steeples, but not having this from creditable eye-witnesses I do not impose upon your faith.

I cannot well omit acquainting you with one manner of fishing used for diversion on this Lough, they take into their boat or cott a goose, and about his body, under his wings, they tie one end of their fishing line, the hook being covered with some bait at the other, thus they throw the fishing-goose into the water, who sports and preens himself with seeming pleasure enough, until some unmannerly fish seizes the baited hook and interrupts her diversions by giving her a tug which douces her almost under water, this commonly frightens her so as to put her to the wing, but if the fish be heavy she is forced to float upon the water, and though in romance the knight generally slays the giant, yet if the pike be of the larger sort Mrs. Goose without the assistance of the spectators is sometimes like to go down to the pike instead of the pike coming up to her.

And now I am speaking of this sort of fish give me leave to tell you a true story concerning the voracity of it, from whence in Latin it is called the water-wolf. A gentleman whom I know and whose word I dare rely upon assured me that as he was fishing for pike in a river called Brosnach in this county he hooked a pretty large one which required some play in the water before he could pull him out without hazard of breaking his tackle, but when he found his fish more manageable and thought he had almost tired him, of a sudden and much to his surprise he found the weight of it mightily increased, which after some wary skill he pulled out of the river and saw the pike which he had hooked half swallowed up by another larger fish of the same kind, who was so very greedy of his prey, or so incapable of disengaging himself from it that both fell into the fisher's hands.

Mullingar in the late war was made a magazine by the English for the army which quartered on that frontier, some slight works were thrown up about it, but such as were very defenceless against any attack ; from hence to Ballymore ten miles through a lovely sheepwalk stocked with a very large English breed of sheep : this a small village considerable for nothing unless for a few days stop which a small fort the Irish had there gave our army in the year '91 ; from hence to Athlone are ten miles more through a country that would delight an Englishman with its prospect.

Athlone is a town standing upon the Shannon and a pass between the Province of Connaught and Leinster, one part of the town which is walled, and the church are in Leinster, another part and the castle are in the province of Connaught. In the year '89 the King sent some forces under the command of Lieut. General Douglas to take in this town but whether it were that they were insufficient for such a work, or that his Majesty had occasion for them at the then siege of Limerick, they decamped soon after their first appearance before it ; the year following the walled town which is on Leinster side was taken by storm and the Irish retired over the bridge into that part of the town which is in Connaught side.

The stream of the river is here rapid and deep, in which stands a large and fair stone bridge. I could not but there admire the hand of the Almighty which gave the English so much strange resolution to attack through this river the works which the Irish had on its banks on the Connaught side, and the success which they had in beating the enemy from them, and becoming masters of a place which the French general might easily have secured, had he not thought it by the most exact rules of war a thing impracticable, and wholly impossible to have address to attempt anything upon them through so many great and unsurmountable difficulties, and because I believe the relation of it will not be unpleasing to you take it thus out of Storye's History of the war of Ireland. . . .

[Following the extract from Story to which Dunton refers comes an amusing but very coarse anecdote about two priests which I omit for the reason given in my introductory note.]

Before I leave this place I cannot forbear taking notice of a mistake of Mr. Eachard's in his exact description of Ireland, where he makes Athlone a Bishopric, which it never was, since the Reformation the Connaught part of it lying in the Bishopric of Elphin, and Leinster part in the diocese of Meath, both which by the bye Mr. Eachard has omitted among the Bishoprics of Ireland.

The county of Westmeath gives the title of earl to one of the Nugents, who is descended from some of the first English who came into this country, they are now Roman Catholics; and Athlone is made an earldom by his present Majesty for the Lord Ginkle who was General at the time of reducing it, and he is Viscount of Aghrim, where the decisive battle was fought the same summer between us and the Dear Joys.

From hence I continued my journey through an uneven rough country towards Galway, here the miles lengthen very much as the country grew worse, as if the badness of the commodity made the inhabitants there afford better measure. At the end of ten miles I came to a place called Ballinasloe, which has nothing remarkable in it. Here the River Suck divides the counties of Galway and Roscommon, three miles beyond this town is Aghrim, an obscure village consisting of few cabins and an old castle, but now made famous by the defeat of St. Ruth and the Irish army; the bones of the dead which lie yet to be seen would make a man take notice of the place. Tis said the Irish here lost 7000 men with their whole camp and all their cannon, whilst the whole loss of the English did not exceed 1000. This which I am very well assured of is very strange. After the battle the English did not tarry to bury any of the dead but their own, and left those of the enemy exposed to the fowls of the air, for the country was then so uninhabited that there were not hands to inter them. Many dogs resorted to this aceldama where for want of other food they fed on man's flesh, and thereby became so dangerous and fierce that a single person could not pass that way without manifest hazard. But a greyhound kept close by the dead body of one who was supposed to have been his master night and day, and though he fed upon other corpses with the rest of the dogs, yet he would not allow them nor anything else to touch that which he guarded.

When the corpses were all consumed the other dogs departed, but this used to go every night to adjacent villages for food and return presently to the place where the beloved bones lay, for all the flesh was consumed by putrefaction, and thus he continued from July till January following, when a soldier passing that way near the dog, who perhaps feared a disturbance of what he so carefully watched, he flew upon the soldier, who shot him with his piece.

From hence to Athenry are fifteen miles through no very delightful country; in it is a wood through which the road lies which affords one remarkable story of the cunning of a fox as that I now acquainted you with the love of a dog. A country fellow who used to carry fresh herrings from Galway to Athlone and those parts of the country had made this his constant road, his fish he used to carry in two wicker baskets without covers, hanging on each side of his horse; one day as he had entered a little into the wood he found a fox lying in the way as if he were dead, and as such he took him by the legs and threw across his horses back with his head in one basket and his hinder legs in the other, secure enough of his skin in the evening, thus he trudged on leading his horse until he had almost gone through the wood, when on some occasion or other, he turned back and missed his fox, which he thought had slipped off, but looking into the baskets they were almost emptied of the fish, the poor fellow surprised searched the bottoms of them and found they were whole and unbroken he then tied his beast to a bush and went hastily back where he saw his herrings scattered up and down in the highway but he never recovered them all, for Mr. Reynard had conveyed several into some of his own privacies; so various are the undoubted instances of the sagacity of beasts, that I can almost believe such a thing as this might have been, and because many of them are endowed with something very like reason, though some people would be very angry at giving it that name, which they suppose the effect only of an immortal soul.

When King John came into Ireland to reduce some of his rebellious people here, he built the town of Athenry, and environed it with a good stone wall to be a curb upon them in those parts. A mile or two from you it makes a great figure, but like most other ill things it shows best at a distance, for when you are in it 'tis a poor, pitiful miserable place, full of cabins and several ruined stone houses and castles; I guess it was once a considerable place, for it has a Tholsel or Town house. This town gives the title of Baron to one Bermingham who is the first of that degree of nobility in Ireland.

Galway is eight miles from hence; about Athenry are delicate sheep walks for near two miles, but all the rest of the way is rocky and barren; Galway is an ancient town and has been of very considerable trade with Spain and France, but now there are not so many merchants among them. I do not take upon me to give you any military account of the place and its fortifications, but this I can tell you, the inhabitants are generally Irish papists, but few protestants besides the soldiery quartered there which commonly are one regiment.

Eachard's mistakes:—I do not find that this place was a bishop's see since the Reformation, though in this present parliament the Archbishop of Tuam endeavoured to procure an Act for removing the cathedral of the archiepiscopal see hither, but could not prevail; however Mr. Eachard is certainly very much out when he reckons this place among the cities of Ireland, for by the records both in Surveyor General's and Auditor General's offices it is called Villa Galviae or the town of Galway. It is governed by a mayor and sheriffs, Lieut. General Bellasis is the present governor though he be in England.

This town gives the title of earl and viscount to Henry Massu marquess Ruvigny, who is now one of the Lords Justices and Lieut. General of the army in this Kingdom.

There were three handsome monasteries here but they are utterly demolished; the town has one large church dedicated to Saint Nicholas. It has some bells in it which are a great rarity in all the country churches here. The houses of this town are all strongly built of stone arched withinside and floored to the uppermost stories with clay, except in some few houses where they use boards for flooring; the transoms to their windows are stone also instead of iron or wood, so that the inside looks like a close prison. It has a pretty quay, and vessels of good burthen lie so near it that one may easily step into them.

The tract of land westward to this near the sea is called Ireconnaught, a wild mountainous country in which the old barbarities of the Irish are so many and so common, that until I came hither, I looked for Ireland in itself to no purpose.

Letter No. 2

As in the body naturall the crisis of the disease is often made by throwing the peccant humor into the extreame parts, soe here the barbarities of Ireland under which it so long laboured, and with which it was soe miserably infected, are all accumulated, and only want the powerfull meanes which drove them from the rest of the kingdom to extirpate them hence also, I meane the planting of English among them, for it is by example mens lives and practises are better reformed than by precept, which seldom prevailes let the charmer charme never so wisely.

Ireconaught lyes west of Galway : on one side it is environ'd by the sea and on the other by the county of Mayo ; it is a mountainous rough country : on the top of the mountaines are boggy grounds, and in most of the vallies lye bogg, loughs and woods some of which have good timber among them, but of the less use because of the difficultye to carry it out of the country.

Six miles beyond Galway is a place called Lynches Folly from the extravagant design of the oner, who endeavour'd to raise a mount in his garden to such an height as to overtop an high mountaine at the foot of which it is situate, soe as to have a veiw of the sea and the neighboureing country ; and he had raised it to considerable height, but by devoureing time it is much crumbled down ; here I tooke a country fellow for a guide, without whom it was absolutely impossible for me to travell further into this country ; I was also well stored with tobacco, cutt and drye, a thing they preferr to meate and drink, and which made me a welcome guest wherever I came, for in these mountaines there are no inns, nor indeed any roads ; my guide was a gentleman descended of one who had been a master of some estate, but the sins of his father in rebellion fell upon him, and often sett his teeth on edge in a litterall sence with eateing sorrell and such trash for want of better food ; he had been a soldier in the late warr, but better advised than many others of his country men he chose rather to stay at home with Prashagh and Potatoes than hazard himself in France where he knew not that any such food grew; the first day towards evening we lost our way, and were forced to lye under the skye that night : I had with me a pocket bottle of usque bagh or aqua vitae, a dram of which and a pipe of tobacco regalled him sufficiently, and with this treatment he was soe well satisfyed that he never complain'd of his lodgeing, haveing been often used to such before. But for me I had been starved, but that he had a tinder-box with which he stroke fire and lighted his sponke, which is the white film groweing on the lower part of the colts foot leafe, which they peal of, and drying it, becomes verie good tinder ; with this he kindled his pipe and some withered grass, and drye osiers, which was to me no small comfort in that cold place ; the next morning when the day appear'd we betooke ourselves to our horses againe, and travelled but a little way on the side of a mountaine before we started an hare in the long grass. My guide happned to have a grey hound with him, the only mark of his gentility, which presently snapt poore puss, who became a supper to us that night, for until then we never had sight of any cabbin ; in the evening we came to a place where one of my guides relations dwelt. There where seaven or eight little hutts together, and the inhabitants haveing spyed us came all bolting out of theire holes to stare at us ; at the place where we alighted the people of the house swept it immediately, and gave us a reception fuller of humanity that I could hope for from persons appearing so barbarous ; some of them brought in back burdens of rushes, green and fresh cutt, with which they made a long thing like a bed to repose my selfe on ; I distributed some tobacco among them which highly obliged them. My guide was my interpreter, and I asked for some water to drinke, but the woman of the house tooke a square wooden vessell called a meddar all of one-piece cutt out of a tree ; and putting some soure milke in it, into which she dipt her nasty fingers twice or thrice to pick out some dirt, she carryed it to a cow for they were all before their doores, and with the milk made me a syllibub, which they call troander ; I was surprized at the pleasing taste and extraordinary coldness of it, on such a sudden.

I layd me down upon my couch of rushes to repose my selfe and desir'd the hare might be gotten ready for supper; I soe much doubted their cookerie that I prayed them to spare them selves the trouble of roasting it; and to let me have it boyld; presently the wife of the house, who was a woman of middle age, well flesht and ruddy complexiond, only a little colour'd with the sun, like one of the mountaine wifes by Juvenal described in his sixth satyr; and indeed the Saturnian time was but a nasty one if as he describes it were true, Dum frigida parvas praeberet spelunca domuis[1] ignemque laremque. Et pecus et dominum communi clauderet umbra, as by this night's experience I found which after supper I shall acquaint you with. My landlady then presently tooke out an old drye horse's hide and layd it on the floore, upon which she placed her querns betwixt her leggs which were naked, and stripping up her clothes to the bottom of her belly which exposed her thighs bare as her face, she opened a small bagg of about three pecks of dried oats and fell to grinding verie lustily. At first I was unwilling to see, not knowing but the woman's inadvertancy made her expose herself so, because there was not a man in the house but my selfe, and I lay quiet as asleep, but some other men of the neighbourhood comeing in and my guide soone after convinced me, that either her greate impudence, or greater innocence made her in that posture without any other concern.

This relation brings into my mind a storie out of Fiens Morison agreeable hereunto. . . . [Here Dunton repeats the well-known and absurd description of O'Kane's daughters]

I assure you my Sabine blouse gave me no such emotions, but rather turned my stomach to what she was prepareing for my supper. When she had ground her oates upon the querns or hand mill-stones, with a little water she made a triangular cake which she reard up before the fire against a little wodden stool made like a tripod, the bakeing of which was committed to the care of her mother, an old woman who was all the while either cramming, sneezeing into her nose or wipeing away the snivell with the same hands that she turn'd my oaten cake, which made my gutts wamble. But alass, this was not all, for my landlady, after she had acquitted herselfe of the cake, fell to washing her hands and

[1] Recte: domos.

arms, and immediately brings to the hearth a small wodden churn, narrow at the mouth and bottle-bellied. She seates her in the same posture as when at the querns, with the churn between her leggs, and claps in her right arm almost up to the arm pitt, which she made use of it instead of a churn staff, and as the milke flasht out of the vessell upon her thighs she stroakt it of with her left into it againe ; the butter was not long comeing, nor do I wonder that Irish butter should smel rank and strong if all be made after this manner, for surely the heate which this labour put the good wife in must unavoidabley have made some of the essence of arms pitts tricle down her arm into the churn ; at last supper was ready and a long stool brought to my bench of rushes instead of a table. The kind landlady haveing no tablecloath, takes of her kercher or linnen wherewith her head was cover'd, which consisting of two or three yards was lapt severall times round about it and hung down in a point halfe way her back, and haveing smothed the wrinekles with her hands as well as she could she layd that before me. It was still warm, which you may judge, afforded no verie pleaseing odour at mealetime. Well the oaten cake was sett next to me, at the lower end of our stoole or table was placed a greate roll of fresh butter of three pound at least, and a wodden vessell full of milk and water. Then enters landlady's daughter with her haire finely plaited, and a blew and red list about her head. In her hand she brought the hare swimming in a wodden boul full of oyl of butter. I told my guide they were verie generous in affording so much sauce to the drye meate, but he answer'd me that was but the broath for they had boyld it in butter and in another cabbin ; you may believe what my appetite was to this dish, and indeed to the whole meale ; I pretended weariness and desired an egg which the daughter presently gott ready. I envited the family to sitt down with my guide, who else were all in waiting. Thus they devour'd the hare and I my eggs which was the only thing I could eate after the sluttish preparations I had been wittness of ; well, drink I must, tho what I had seen made me nauseate everie vessell, but I was under too greate a necessity to forbeare. I sett my meddar to my head, and shut my eyes, not to preserve them as some doe when they drink, but for feare of makeing any ungratefull discoveries in my liquor, which I powr'd down eagerly enough that I might be the sooner ridd of it. At the verie last I found between my teeth a long straw, you may guess at what it almost occasion'd. My guide told me by way of excuse it was nothing but a piece of the streiner, and no hurt in it. This put me upon enquireing how they streind their milk and to satisfye me the engine was brought to us, which was a round thing made of the bark of a birch tree of a conical figure and stuffed with cleane straw or grass, and through this they let theire milke run, by which haires and dirt are separated from it. Thus supper ended and I made a dole of my tobacco to everieone againe, which they received with all the expressions of gratitude they could shew. I now desired to be at rest. The landlord and my guide reached down a greate and long bagg which was hanging at one of the rafters of the house, out of which the wife tooke two verie large and white and soft bundles of woollen by them called Breadeen, thinner than their friezes and thicker than our flannel. These were layd upon my rushes and glad of such a cleane and warm covering, where I expected not any atal, I put of my cloaths the verie women not turning aside theire heads, and lapt myself in my woollen blankets which indeed were the only cleane things I mett with in this Country.

I had but just compos'd my selfe to sleep when I was strangely surprized to heare the cows and sheep all comeing into my bed chamber. I enquired the meaneing and was told it was to preserve them from the wolfe which everie night was rambling about for prey. I found the beasts lay down soone after they had enter'd and soe my feares of being trodden upon by them were over; and truly if the nastiness of theire excrements did not cause an aversion hereto, the sweetness of theire breath which I never was sensible of before, and the pleaseing noyse they made in ruminating or chawing the cudd, would lull a body to sleep as soon as the noys of a murmuring brook and the fragrancy of a bed [of] roses.

The next morning a greate pott full of new milk was sett over the fire, and when it was hott they pour'd into it a pale full of butter milk, which made a mighty dish of tough curds in the middle of which they placed a pound weight of butter, but the unusualness of the mess and the sluttishness of the cookery kept me from eateing any of it; I proffered them mony at my goeing away for my entertainment, but they refus'd it with some marks of displeasure because they were of the gentry which until then I was ignorant of. However I prevaild upon them to accept of some tobacco, which they did with thanks. At takeing my leave my landlady and her daughter, for I saw not the old woman, came to me, and clapping theire hands to my eares by way of embrace, kissed me and gave me theire blessing spitting lightly upon my cloaths.[2]

From hence we journeyed through the same sort of country soe boggy that in many places we were forced to lead our horses. Mine lost all his shoes and no smith to shoe him, but the soyl was soe far from hard, that it did his hoofes no hurt ; nor doe any in these parts shoe theire horses at all, and their hoofes are so hard and tough (that as they did informe me) they did not require shoeing when they travelled into countryes of an harder soyl ; here are numerous loughs or lakes but none of any greate biggness, about which are thousands of otters to be seen, and some verie large and almost black. Att first I tooke them for some other creatures till my guide enform'd me what they were, and as soone as ever they espyed us they plung'd into the water and disappear'd. They are creatures when taken young that grow verie docill and may easily be made verie good fishers, bringing the fish which they catch in the water to their master standing upon the bank. I know a gentleman who had an otter of his one trayneing that brought him more then three score trouts out of a river in one evening. He enform'd me that when they fish in rivers they always swim against the streame, and soe come behind the fish and surprize it, for the trout lyes in the current with his nose pointing against it in expectation of worms or other food which it frequently carryeth with it, as the gentleman has frequently observ'd ; but how they fish in standing pools like these loughs he could not enforme me.

A gentleman in Galway to whom I was recommended by one who was friend to us both in Dublin gave me his recommendatorye letters to one O'Flaghertie the most considerable man in this territorye. He was son to one Sir Murragh na Mart O Flaghertie ; the name of na Mart

---

[2] It is unlikely that this is pure invention on Dunton's part, though I have never met any other evidence corroborating it.

was added uppon the occasion of his killing and devoureing in his one house, among his servants and followers everye Shrove Tuesday at night fifty beefes, and this I am told of the Irish papists in generall that the eve of their Lent they doe lay in a greate deale of flesh, gormandizeing that night enough to serve them untill Easter, at which time they rise early in the morning to swallow down more of their beloved flesh; but this you must take notice of in the vulgar and poorer sort of people, not among the gentry. This gentleman was among a greate company of his relations, as being the chiefe of the clan or family, when I arrived at his house, which was a long cabbin, the walls of hurdles plaister'd with cow dung and clay. I produced my credentialls and was civilly received. They were a parcell of tall lusty fellows with long haire, straite and well made, only clumsy in their leggs, theire ankles thicker in proportion to their calves than the English, which is attributed to theire weareing broags without any heels ; but this I leave to the learned. The men after the old Irish fashion as well as the weomen weore theire haire verie long, as an ornament, and to add to it the weomen commonly on Saturday night, or the night before they make their appearance at mass or any publick meeting doe wash it in a lee made with stale urine and ashes, and after in water to take away the smell, by which their locks are of a burnt yellow colour much in vogue among them.

My treatment here was much as the night before, only there was a mutton killed for supper, half of which was boyld and the other roasted, and all devour'd at the meale. After supper the priest, who as I suppose was as a sort of chaplaine to the family called for tables to play for an half-pennorth of tobacco, but was reprimanded by the lady of the house for doeing it before he had return'd thankes, and civilly enquired of me if I understood the game. My being ignorant of it made them lay it aside. I made the priest a present of my tobacco which was wellcome to them all ; even the lady herself bore them company in smoakeing and excus'd it by urgeing the need they were in of some such thing in that moist country, which I could not contradict. I enquired about the customs of ploweing by their horses tayl, and burning the corn in the straw. They told me the former was wholy disused as a thing too injurious, their cattle often loosing their tayls thereby, but they still burn their corn to save themselves the trouble of thrashing, soe that in one houres time you may see the sheaves taken out of the stack and burnt, the corn winnowed ground on theire querns and made bread for the table. This Mr. Oflaghertie had converst among the English, had been at Dublin and was sensible enough of their one barbarous way in liveing, but sayd it was a thing soe habituall to them that it could not be suddainly removed. He told me that the high sheriff of the county which is Galway came thither with a design to put the statutes in execution against those who plowed by the tayl or burnt their corn, and comeing one night to lye at the house of one of those gentlemen there present (for you must know the Irish are all gentlemen, tho beggars and vagabonds, if they be of a name that has ever a gentleman of it), supper was gotten ready and lay'd on the table, and at the sherif's side on a stoole were placed halfe a dozen sheaves of oates ; which he enquireing the meaneing of, was told, they were unprovided of bread and durst not burn their corn before him, but such as they had he was welcome to ; the sherif was hungry and more desirous of filling his belly at that time than of putting the laws in execution, and soe was contented to see the corn burnt to provide bread for his breakfast. One thing I saw in this hous perhaps the like not to be seen anywhere else in the world, and that was nine brace of wolfe doggs or the long Irish grey hounds, a paire of which kind has been often a present for a king, as they are said to be a dog that is peculiar to Ireland, for I am told they breed much better here than any where else in the kingdom. They were as quiet among us as lambs without any noys or disturbance. I enquir'd the use of them and was told that besides the ornament that they were, they kill'd as many deer as pay'd verie well for their keeping, and they promis'd to oblidge me next day by letting me see how they caught their game. I discover'd some apprehensions of dread to lye among such a number of monsters if they were permitted within doores all night, but they had a cabbin for their kennell, and were brought in at supper time only to surprize me with the noveltie. I am well assur'd that a dog of this kind which my Lord Duke of Ormond had in the castle of Dublin when he was Lord Liut. walkt into the stable yard where a little curr kept a barking and yelping at him, which he never regaurded but walkt forward with a careless pace, untill the curr snapt him by the heeles, which made the grehound give him a patt with his fore foot which layd him on the ground, and then standing over him pist upon him; the same dog being provokt by a small setting dogg which belongd to the Duke tooke him by the back and layd him gently upon a coale fire in the state roome and walked unconcernedly away.

The house was one entire long roome without any partition. In the middle of it was the fire place with a large wood fire which was no way unpleaseing tho in summer time. It had no chimney but a vent hole for the smoake at the ridge, and I observ'd the people here much troubled with sore eyes; which I attributed to the sharp smoak of the wood, and they also allowed it but sayd they had newly put up this for a Booley or summer habitation, the proper dwelling or mansion house being some miles farther neare the sea, and such an one they commonly built everie yeare in some one place or other, and thatch'd it with rushes or coarse grass as this was; we all lay in the same roome upon green rushes. I had sheets and soft white blankets which they emulate one another in verie much (I meane the housewives among them), and they assur'd me no man ever gott cold by lyeing on green rushes, which indeed are sweet and cleane, being changed everie day if raine hinders not; but tho they have not lice among them, they are verie full of white snayles which I found upon my cloaths. I wonder'd mightily to heare people walking to the fire place in the middle of the house to piss there in the ashes, but I was soone after forced to doe soe too for want of a chambrepot, which they are not much used unto . . . (Here follows a story in the manner of Balzac, apropos of this.)

But to leave this digression, the next morning earely after a large breakefast of six wodden bowls filled with hott flesh meate which I could not taste, and a drachm of theire bulcaan or worse sort of aqua vitae, Oflaghertie invited me to walk a small mile to view theire deer. I willingly consented because I did not expect to heare of Deer Park in so wild a place; we walked over mountains and through boggs, thro thick and thin, sometimes out and sometimes in untill I lost the heels of my shoos, which tyred me soe that I thought I should never come to the miles end, which was modestly speakeing as farr as half way from Whitehall to Barnet. At last we came to [a] pleasant vale called Glinglass, or the Green Vale, of an English miles breadth encompasst with lovely green mountaines which were tufted with pleasant groves and thickets of natures provideing, for none here imitate her in ought but her coarser draughts; on the sides of these hills I wonder'd to see some hundreds of stately red deer, the stags bigger than a large English yeareling calfe, with suitable antlers much bigger than any I ever saw before.

It was the most pleaseing scene that ever I met with in this kingdom, and the only thing worth my notice in these parts. We return'd before the heate of the day to our greate cabbin, where we had at dinner, no less then a whole beef boyl'd and roasted, and what mutton I know not so profewsly did they lay it on the table. At the upper end where the lady sate was placed an heap of oaten cakes above a foot high, such another in the middle and the like at the lower end; at each side of the middle heap were placed two large vessels filled with Troander or the whey made with buttermilk and sweet milk, which being about two days old was wonderfull cold and pleaseing in that hott time of the day. We had ale (such as it was) and Bulcaan, and after dinner myn host ordered his doggs to be gotten ready to hunt the stagg. He had his horse saddled and one for me too, because the loss of my heels render'd me incapable of such a walk. Eighteen long greyhounds and above thirty footemen made up the company. We were not long before we arriv'd at Glinglass, our horses in a manner galloping over the boggs and hills, for I rode one of his, it being unpracticable to mine to goe fast on such ground. Our foote company kept close to our horses and the grey hounds did sometimes putt themselves into a trott which was noble and greate; the hills which before were cover'd with red deer were now quite empty and not one to be seen. It seems in the heat of the day they retire into covert and lye there untill towards evening. Oflaghertie gave the word and immediately the company with the doggs surrounded a large thicket, whilst he and I with two hunting poles enter'd it to rouze the game. The first we saw was a stately stagg who secure of daunger skipped forth of the bushes; he at first seem'd amazed at the cry which was raised looing the doggs, but he bravely endeavour'd charge through them, and was seized by one of the dogs at the haunch, which threw him on his back. The whole kenel was not suffer'd to come in for feare of spoyleing the skin which the people most value, and never did I see a spanniell more subject to command than those mighty dogs are; I desir'd the next might have more play for his life; accordingly the doggs were all taken up, and the next proveing a stagg too broke through the men who did not let slip more than a brace of their doggs. It was indeed a noble course for a little way, but the stagg tooke a leap out of our sight from a prominent part of the hill into the valley where the doggs lost. After we had done beateing this thicket, where we rouzed two brace, three of which we kill'd, after the same manner, I went to view the leap which the stagg made that escapt. It seem'd to me as high as a steeple, and the deere was not kill'd by the fall. After this afternoones diversion we return'd home where to beef and mutton we had venison, boyld and roasted, and a fish call'd a Loggerhead by them. It was a firm white fish of good taste and as a bigg as a salmon, but how to describe it they could not tell, and I saw not any but that one, which I could not observe to any purpose of description.

Beyond this place towards the county of Mayo lyes Buffin neare the sea, which gave after the abdication the title of Barron to one of the late Earle of Clonricards sons, whom the English doe not stile soe because it was conferrd on him since the late King left England. The Isles of Arran, which give the title of Earle to the Earle of Arran, the Duke of Ormond's brother, lye of this continent; they are three in number and in the middlemost of them there is a fort and a company of soldiers commonly lye there in garrison. The accountt of these islands I only have by hearesay, for the country was soe wild and destitute of conveniencyes of life it hindred my further progress.

By what I have observ'd here, which most resembles old Ireland of any part of the kingdom, I take the Irish to be a people well humor'd and open hearted, and verie capable of good impressions if a prudent care be taken to manage them. Indeed their religion is a greate obstacle hereunto, but this is not only to be imputed to them, for we heare of the horrid barbarities dayly, which the French soe polite a people commit upon their countrymen, nay neighbours and for ought I know relations too ; their nastines and ignorance are to be imputed to their poverty and want of conversation, and this is much occasion'd by that, for such of them as have competent fortunes to support them shew enough of conversible humor. What they are in their trafick and dealeings I cannot tell otherwise than by common fame which I am loath to credit. I shall conclude this with a relation soe credibly delivered me that I cannot doubt but that among these despicable Irish there was a man as much to be celebrated as Quintus Cincinnatus in Rome.

My Irish hero (for I cannot call a man of his character by a less name) was of the Reylys in the county of Cavan. His circumstances were verie meane and obscure, tho his father had an handsom estate in that county which he forfeited by the rebellion of fourty one ; he among the rest was restor'd to his father's forfeitures by their pretended Parliament and became a Liut. Coll. of foot. He always exprest a greate care of the English, and protected their persons and goods upon all occasions, soe that many were obliged to him for their preservation. He followed the fate of his country men all the course of the warr, and when Limrick was surrendered his regiment was one of those which went to France. Some English gentlemen of our army who knew what he done for the English whenever it lay in his way, diswaded him from leaveing his native country, where he had deserv'd so well of those who might be suddenly be in a condition to make him a suitable return for his kindnesses ; he answer'd that he had embarqued what little he had in his country's cause, that all was lost, and he had rather begg or starve among strangers than he reduc't to such necessityes among those who had soe lately seen him make some tollerable figure. To this the gentlemen answer'd they soe well knew how generous he was to them and their neighbours when it was in his power to doe otherwise, and when it was become necessary for men in his post to shew their zeale to their cause by some cruell proofs, that they would then enter into engagements to procure him a comfortable subsistance from the government or if that faild they would advance it out of theire one estates which he knew were competent enough. The Irishman told them with teares in his eyes how sensibly their generosity toutcht him, and therefore he thought him selfe oblidg'd to refuse it, else his past actions which they soe kindly resented, might seem to have been by way of secureing himself a retreate in extremity, which was farr from his heart, and therefore thought himselfe sufficiently rewarded by the kind intentions they discover'd towards him ; and soe tooke his leave, and was never heard of since, that I could learne.

Letter No. 3

Whether religion be practised among other Roman Catholics as it is among the Irish I am yet to learn, but surely if it be, the ignorance of their clergy and people must be the cause of it. More appearance of devotion among the laity at celebration of their mass is not everywhere to be found, but yet so full of a blind zeal that the poor wretches know nothing of what they do or say. For while the Pater is repeating from their altar, you shall hear others thumping their breasts and muttering an Ave Maria, the Credo, or Mea culpa, as my own senses assure me. In short the main of their religion consists in a blind and total adhering to what is delivered to them by their oracles their clergy ; but this is chiefly to be observed among the poorer and illiterate people ; for some of them who have found the advantages of a liberal education are ashamed of the ignorance and impudence of their priesthood, and have as little regard to them on that score, as the theistical witty gentlemen in England have for the ministry there on another account. Though one of these who would not own himself a stranger to either sense or learning, being at the house of a person whom I very well know, took a large church bible with bosses and clasps which he found on a table and looking into the Chronicles was much taken with the history of those wars which he chanced to fall upon, and desired to borrow the book ; which the other consented to on condition he would read it through. Dear joy promised he would ; he was then desired to look into the title page, and finding it to be what it was, he let it fall to the ground, and full of confusion withdrew himself from it protesting it was unawares he was guilty of the crime of reading in it, and that he could not with a safe conscience conceal it from his ghostly father at next confession, and thus you may see how the waters of life are conveyed to these poor people, through the hands of vile and designing clergy not allowing them to approach the sacred fountain themselves.

I shall then begin with their way of initiation of children into their religion, and I hope I may be allowed this, as well as others, are the accounts of such things among Indians or other remote nations; for though these be things daily used among us in England as well as here, yet perhaps few know the ceremonies extracted out of the Roman Missal published by the command of Pope Paul the Fifth for the use of England, Scotland and Ireland. I shall therefore here premise something of the labours or delivery of their women with child, not that it is a thing I was ever present at, but as what was delivered to me by serious relations both of English and Irish.

And surely if the curse laid upon Eve to bring forth her children in sorrow has missed any of her posterity, it must be here, many of the poorer and laborious sort of the women bearing their children without any long labour or extreme pains as among others, nay even without the assistance of other women, often proving their own midwives; though when they fall into any great distress as sometimes they do, the barbarities they are often used with, by those who call themselves their assistants are such as would make a reasonable man believe they were used to frustrate the very intentions of nature, such as plunging the woman when her labour is long or difficult into a pit of cold water, or laying her upon their cold earthen floor; and if these means prove unsuccessful they take a rope and fastening it about the infant's neck, they pull and haul it until either they deliver the woman or pull off the child's head, which they sometimes happen to do. They also have a custom to wrap the labouring woman in their husband's coat, and as the delivery proves either easy or difficult, they form fancies of the man's being a good or bad husband.

For the ease that generally they are delivered with I think a reason may be probably assigned, and that is the loose and unconstrained dress they wear and labour which they use, whereby their bodies are rendered very apt for distention. The famous Dr. Harvey gives one instance of them by a woman who following her husband in the army felt her labour coming on, went under a hedge, bore her child, carried to some water where she washed it, wrapped it up in her mantle, and so trudged on until night, without anyone knowing her delivery. Before I left Ireconnaught Mr. O'Flagherty, mentioned in my last, carried me to a christening where he was gossip ; I was much surprised to see the mother delivered but two days before about the house, but not suffered to touch either any of the meat or drink provided for the guests, because they deem her unhallowed until her churching or Purification be performed. After some large draughts of Bulkcan which they poured merrily down, the ceremony began according to the before-mentioned missal.

The infant being brought to the church door (for want of churches this is to be done at the door of the chamber where it is baptized), but that was here dispensed with the whole house being one room, the priest meets it clad in his vestments, he asketh the gossips what seek they from the church of God ; to which they answer Faith . . .

I have here forborne any remarks of my own and have stuck to the literal translation,[1] which I leave to everyone to consider how extravagant it is, and surely surprising enough to those who are unacquainted therewith, and for aught I see every jot as strange as several customs used religiously among the Georgians or Aethiopians. I remembered at this occasion what Mr. Eachard mentions in his second chapter of his Exact Description of Ireland (which as a historian he many places fails in, as I shall have several instances to produce), that when they are baptized they commonly add some profane name taken from an event, colour, etc. Now here I am positive no such thing was mentioned, and if anywhere in Ireland, these parts I think are most likely to find it in, as retaining so much of its ancient barbarous customs ; as also another mistake of his, that they never give the name of the living father or any of the relations then living because it is unlucky, of which this place may serve for an instance, where the christened child was called Brian, from his godfather Brian O'Flagherty, though it was the name of the child's father too. And this I have since enquired after and find it not taken notice of in several places where the children are called after the fathers and mothers

[1] This is omitted here : see introductory remarks at beginning of Appendix B. It is a straightforward but not first hand description of a christening. There is nothing 'extravagant' or offensive about it.

names. When they grow up it is true they are called Oge or young (if the parent be living) as a mark of distinction, and for such reason it is that the Agnomen or what he calls the Profane Name is added, a thing used among the Romans and our very English too, as William the Conqueror, Henry of Monmouth etc.; but to return whence that gentleman's mistake has made me digress.

After the ceremony of baptism was over we had four persons who fell to play on their Jews Trumps, each playing on two at once. The music was no way disagreeable, but most of their airs were melancholy and doleful as suiting the humours of a people always in subjection. We had no plum-cakes nor sweet meats, but vast quantities of flesh, milk, butter, and Bulcaan. We stayed not all night, as others did, to devour all the victuals, as on such occasions they commonly do, not leaving to the family common supplies for the next day.

Their gossipred is a thing in a manner sacred among them, and nothing so effectually puts an end to differences between families (or at least no greater sign can be given of their reconciliation), than in being gossips to one the other. Young lovers among them avoid being partners at a christening (where they have but one godfather and one godmother), for if they do and marry within a year and a day 'tis counted ominous.

I was here told a story of an Irish gentleman being invited to a great feast, where there was to be a cosher at night, that is where all the guests with their retinue lie in the same room upon straw or rushes and pig together. The gentleman had some other avocations but that it might not be taken ill he sent his wife, and one who was their gossip and then accidentally in the house agreed to accompany her. The careful husband, who it's like had known what pranks are usually played on such occasions, advised his wife to put on a pair of his woollen drawers and to sew up the slit of the codpiece. Accordingly she put them on and went with her gossip to the feast where, after they had filled themselves sufficiently, the coshering place was ready and down they layed rustling together hickledy-pickledy in the dark. If when the belly is full the bones would be at rest you may believe theirs soon put them to sleep. I never heard how honest they all were in that promiscuous lodging, but next day when the good wife and her gossip returned home among other occurrences which the gossip related to the gentleman he told him that, happening to lie by one whom he took for a female, he made bold to satisfy his curiosity and found she was asleep and had a pair of woollen drawers on ; that being provoked by the opportunity he drew his skean and with it cut a slit in them fit for his purpose . . . the husband's boding mind did not let him stay any longer until he cleared his fears, but calling his wife to him he presently found who it was his gossip had made a cuckold of ; which was forgiven without any great difficulty, as much perhaps to conceal the disgrace as on account of the gossipred.

I never had an opportunity of seeing any of their weddings, though I never could find them to be as Mr. Eachard in 2nd Chapter speaks of them ; for first there is a set form of matrimony prescribed them in their Roman Missal, which they have too great a veneration for ever to transgress at least with a bare face : secondly adultery or fornication are here as punishable as in England, and the church wardens being Protestants are sworn to make presentations of all such into their respective Bishop's courts ; neither are there any divorces made here but by the spiritual court, that is a vinculo matrimonii ; 'tis true the mutual one a mensa et thoro may be made by the joint consent of the parties and so no more a novelty here than in England, and the English laws are here so duly executed that unless it be in some such remote nook of the kingdom as Ireconnaught (to which Mr. Eachard doth not confine himself) no such thing can be practised but by stealth.

In my return towards Dublin I was benighted near the dwelling of one Mr. B——an Irish gentleman, to whom addressing myself under the circumstances of a benighted stranger, I was civilly received, but with an excuse for the disorder I was to find them in on the account of his mother being near expiring. I know not by what accident I asked had she received the Holy Oil : to which he answered No ; and the question fortunately enough made them guess me one of the same religion too. I seemed cautious as a man in a strange place, though I rather gave him hints to confirm his first apprehensions of my belief than any way alter them. Before supper the priest came to give her the Extreme Unction, and not doubting me a good Catholic as they call themselves, I was admitted to the ceremony, for she had made confession and received absolution some days before.

The priest clothed in his vestments entered the sick woman's chamber (for in this house there were partitions and tolerable rooms) with Peace to this house etc. Then setting the oil on the table he gave her a crucifix to kiss, after which he besprinkled her, the room, and all the bystanders with holy water in form of a cross muttering something which I could not understand, and then fell to give her some spiritual consolations in Irish, which was Hebrew to me ; which being performed he went to prayers. When he had finished them he prepared for giving the unction, and bade us to use some devout prayers in her behalf whilst he was administering that holy sacrament to her. We all fell a muttering, nor did I think myself bowing in the house of Rimmon when I said the Lord's Prayer in Latin ; what the others said I could not tell, being more intent to the priest, though I heartily prayed for an easy exit and an happy futurity to the poor woman.

Thus then he began, saying In the Name of the Father etc. (using three crosses upon the sick), may all the power of the devil be extinguished in thee by the imposition of these our hands, and by the invocation of all holy angels, archangels, patriarchs, prophets, apostles, martyrs, confessors, virgins and all the other saints : Amen. Then dipping his thumb into the oil and making a cross on her eyes he prayed that all the sins she had committed with them might be forgiven her ; then he wiped the besmeared oil from off her eyes with a white cloth, as he did from all the other parts which he annointed, and after the ceremony was over he burned it ; from the eyes he went to the nostrils thence to her lips, then hands, and feet, praying for a forgiveness (or rather giving absolution) for the sins committed by each particular part. Thus after a few prayers he finished his sacrament of Extreme Unction. Which brings to my mind an unfortunate accident which attended one of these operations in Dublin. A poor fellow who drove a hackney coach was so unlucky as to want the help of a surgeon or doctor for a malady not very rare among those who delight in lewd women. The wretch's condition was such that he was put into their powdring tub as they call it and fluxed, and when the course was near its height, and his face and tongue so swelled that he could hardly be understood, one of these priests came to see him (for the fellow was a papist), and finding him in that condition concluded immediately death was at hand, and hastens for his trinkets to perform the Unction with. It happened that not one of them who were about the patient had ever seen a salvation before, and therefore all deemed him desperate and as a lost man. The priest came but could receive no confession, however gave him the unction, and because the disease came from such a sin he omitted not the unction of the penis pronouncing forgiveness to Quicquid per lumborum delectationeum deliquit. In short then the priest was so long at his work that the poor fellow got cold, which so stopped his spitting as caused such a tumour in those parts that suffocated the poor man who before was in no dangerous condition at all.

We had a good supper and not much sorrow among us for the good old gentlewoman, because she was very aged and had been for some time bedrid and as it were dead to the family. However the thoughts of her engaged us in more serious discourse, among which they told me when any of their family was near their end some spectre by them called a Banshee, or fetch, forewarned them of it, and that it had been heard several times of late using a lamentable cry about the house. I found they all believed stories of fairies, hobgoblins, or lemures, and to argue any thing against such beings was all in vain. So much were they prepossessed with the tales received from their forefathers, even the priest himself was of the same mind, though he had nothing more than tradition to confirm what he thought, for he was wholly a stranger to those texts of Holy Writ as are used for arguments in favour of them, nor had he ever troubled his head with Metaphysical notions. And indeed I could not without astonishment behold the mighty ignorance of their illiterate priests, the best of them that I saw having little other marks of common school learning than to tell you of Ovid's Metamorphosy, Virgil or Cicero, the two last of which I am confident their intellects did not allow them to understand. No wonder then that the miserable vulgar are besotted with foolish notions, when those who take upon them the name and office of teachers, are themselves so very mean in their qualifications for it ; nor can it well be otherwise since their church here can give no comfortable subsistence to any that enter upon its functions. So that they who had such estates as capacitated their children for liberal education this way, seeing the small prospect to be had of a future livelihood by it, bestowed them otherways ; by which means those who were the meanest of the people, at least in their fortunes, give their sons so much learning, as they call it, as fit them to construe their mass-book, which is a sufficient qualification for their priesthood ; though some few examples have been found of estated men designing their children for this office, and those they sent into France to study. But these instances are very rare ; it is true some of these illiterate priests do boast of having studied in France, but they had no other means of support there than in being menial servants to some convent ; and yet return home again with great reputation for having been travellers, without considering what improvements they had made.

The old gentlewoman was grown much weaker, and Father Laurence, for so the priest was called, advised to give her her Viaticum which was the sacrament of the Lord's Supper, her death being so very near. I thought I should not meet any more with such an opportunity of satisfying my curiosity. So under the notion they had of me I entered the sick woman's room among the rest. The priest after mumbling something between his teeth, which I supposed prayers, adored the host on his knees, and then lifting it up showed it to [the] sick woman and said, Behold the Lamb of God which taketh away the sins of the world ; then using a short ejaculation he put the wafer into her mouth with these words, take, sister your Viaticum of Christ's body, which may preserve thee from the evil enemy and into eternal life ; thus after a prayer or two more, the office was over, and the woman left to make her exit. . . .

It was now bed time, and I was showed a lodging upstairs, which I had no reason to complain of. But I had not been long asleep before I was wakened by a very loud cry, and opening my eyes, I saw a great light at my window that was streetward. The sight surprised me thinking the house was on fire, and I ran in my shirt to the window where looking out I saw a great bundle of straw before the door on fire, and three or four women clapping their hands, and sending forth the most horrid yells that ever I heard. The reason of this as I was afterwards informed was because of a custom used among them. For at the death of anyone they carry out their bed, which is commonly of straw (or if their condition allow them better, then they get a large bundle of straw), and set it on fire before the door of the house, with such sharp and loud cries as pierced my head quite through, to give notice to the neighbourhood of the decease. The house was not long 'ere filled with abundance of women, and everyone that entered set up the shout, as all in the room did together, after the corpse was washed and stretched out ; like those loud outcries used by the Romans at the death of their friends in hopes to recover them from their deep sleep. For several lethargic and comatose persons have by shouts and loud cries been brought again to themselves when in appearance they were dead ; so that such as were proof against the third experiment were deemed as dead and utterly gone; and for the same cause do these people use the same way. I was next day preparing to take my leave of mine host, but I found it would oblige him if I could stay to wake his mother that night. I had more curiosity than civility or good nature, which induced my stay to see the performances of the wake which I expected to be no less than a rare show ; nor was I frustrated in what I looked for.

After night fall the corpse was carried forth without any shouting or noise into a Great Barn, where at one end was raised an altar by laying an old door upon a couple of barrels. Near this was the corpse placed (without any coffin), covered with a white sheet. All the room was filled with small lighted candles, and seats of green sods made round about, the floor all covered with rushes. Thus what company attended the body seated themselves, where some constrained silence was a little while observed. And everyone that entered at the door made some sign of reverence towards the place where the corpse lay, and kneeling down repeated a Pater Noster or an Ave Maria for the soul of the deceased. About midnight, most of the company being then gathered that was expected to come, great platters of boiled flesh were brought into the barn and abundance of bread, all made in fine white cakes of wheat flour. I do not here mean small cakes like our saffron ones or biscuits, but of size as large as a sieve and near three inches thick, portions of which with flesh was distributed to every one of the people, and great tubs of drink which was brewed that day followed on hand barrows ; with which they filled themselves so that all night they kept an intolerable belching, though I did not hear one make a crack at the other end, so odious is this among them and so little is the other taken notice of. After this dole of victuals was distributed the gentleman with his wife and other relations who were come to him on this occasion, retired to the dwelling house, but I stayed behind among the crowd. And now came tobacco and pipes, and sneezing, and of a sudden I had such a representation of hell as Don Que Vevodo himself never saw. The room, large as it was, soon filled with clouds of smoke, which made the small candles give so faint a light as if they were just going out. The elder sort sat sneezing or belching, whilst a lusty young fellow snatches a kercher (that is the wreath of linen wherewith the women's heads are covered) from her head, and tied it about his hat as a distinguishing mark of his office among them. Then as captain or master of misrule he selected a band of about a dozen young fellows who hauled out so many women of the younger sort for their mates ; and by these were the rudest, most unpolished and barbarous sorts of sports used that ever were seen, especially in such a place where such an object of mortality lay ; to which not one that I saw showed the least regard. Sometimes they followed one another in a ring (as they say fairies do), in a rude dance to the music of a bagpipe, and as a great jest sometimes they made excursions with their nasty houghs upon some old body who may-be was nodding and it passed very well. After this they betook themselves to another sort of play, where one fellow ran his head between the thighs of another and so hoist him on his shoulders whilst a third clapped his buttocks till they were (surely) sore. Wonder not that I cannot give you a more exact account of the Irish behaviour in this place, for several had taken off their brogues, whose filthy odours, joined with those sweaty emanations caused by the heat they were in, were such that, could you form an idea of them, you would rather admire how I could stay so long, or indeed how I was able to come forth alive.

In short, such was the unexpressible rudeness I saw there, that I know not whether I had not as soon suffer a dead friend to be disfigured by rats, as expose him to such unaccountable barbarities ; and if any stranger were to make a judgement of the other customs of the Irish by this one of waking their dead, he might justly reckon them among the rudest and most beastly people in the world. The next day new vast quantities of meat and drink were given among the people. About eleven the last Mass was said for her soul in the barn, where I was told twelve were performed that morning: for now we had six or seven priests. And soon after all their neighbours being come, among whom were many English, the corpse was brought forth (but first let me tell you that I saw about 20 women guzzling usquebagh or aqua vitae ; I enquired who they were, and was told they were the Mna Keena or howling women who had this given them to support their spirits in that laborious work), and an horrid cry was immediately set up where some hundreds joined in the concert. It was such as you cannot conceive nor I express, but such a peal it gave my ears as deprived them for some time of their hearing. The corpse was laid upon a bier in a coffin as among Christians, and one thing which pleased me much was that her children and other relations, I mean the men, carried her on their shoulders, which as it was the last I thought was a very grateful office.

We had not far to go to the burial place which was a ruined church near unto which was an high heap of stones, where the bier was set down and some prayers said, and all I believe that could get a stone threw one into that heap. I found it was because everyone who did so is by old custom to say a short prayer as often as they go by, for the souls of those at whose funerals they threw a stone there. But before we enter the place of burial I protest I saw not one woman with tears in her eyes, though I think more than a hundred were shouting lamentable cries with clapping of hands and all the other expressions of violent sorrow. The corpse was interred with some ceremony, but what it was I could not get near enough to see because of the crowd. And when the company was dispersed, the women betook them to the several graves of their friends and there sat some while mourning over them with a low but very lamentable cry, telling the mishaps that befell them since their death.

It was because I would not interrupt the description of

the funeral preparation and pomp, that I did not take notice of the sermon which Father Laurence was pleased to give us on this occasion. Have you seen the oration that Anthony made at Caesar's obsequies, or any other the most celebrated among the Romans? If you have prepare yourself then to hear one not in the least like anything that is like 'em, and believe it was more to satisfy your curiosity than my own that I was at the trouble to take to it in short-hand.

It was a fair day, and after the last Mass the corpse was brought forth to the barn door where a table was placed for the preacher to mount on. Up gets Father Laurence and after three crosses and a bow to the company he thus began. . . .

[The sermon, which as recorded by Dunton is probably largely his own invention, is of no interest and is therefore omitted.]

Letter No. 4

I had done drinking the waters of Templeoag, which I used about four weeks instead of those of Tunbridge, to which I think these are no way inferior in their taste, diuretic quality, or the other phenomena they afford on pouring galls into them. They lie three small miles from Dublin, at the bottom of a higher ground, near a small river, and in wet weather they grow weak. Few go thither to drink them, there are so many carriers who bring them from thence by five in the morning for a penny a bottle to the city, though the physicians are of opinion that they are stronger at the spring; however they did very well with me.

On Tuesday September the 19th I began my second ramble to Kilkenny. I took a coach to one gent's a mile out of town, where my horse waited for me, and here my good fortune threw me upon the ingenious Clymene who happened to travel that road for some miles. Rachcool [Rathcoole] was the first place we came to; it is a country village with two indifferent inns, and six miles from Dublin. Here we met Clymene's husband and baited a while. In our inn some years since dwelt a woman who murdered her guests that had money with them. It was not long concealed and she was burned for the fact. Here I saw something I never saw since my coming into the country, and that was several little children as naked as ever they were born easing themselves on the dunghills before the doors of the cabins. From hence to Naas are six miles more. This is a good handsome town with several good stone houses, and two handsome taverns besides, several inns, a large church and session house where the assizes are held, it being the shire-town of the county of Kildare and a borough sending two members to the Parliament whose names now are Nevil and Barry. The inhabitants of this place and the neighbourhood have a custom (how begun I could not learn) on Shrove Tuesday to meet on horseback in the fields, and wherever they spy a hare in her form, they make as wide a circle as the company can and the ground will permit, and someone is sent in to start poor puss, who cannot turn herself any way but she is repulsed with loud cries and so frightened that she falls dead in the magical circle, though sometimes she breaks through and escapes, if a greyhound or any other dog be found in the field, it is a thousand to one he loses his life; and thus after they have shouted two or three hares to death they disperse.

And now I think I may say something to you of the sports used among the Irish on their holidays. One exercise they use much is their hurling, which has something in it not unlike the play called Mall. When their cows are casting their hair, they pull it off their backs and with their hands work it into large balls which will grow very hard. This ball they use at the hurlings, which they strike with a stick called commaan about three foot and a half long in the handle. At the lower end it is crooked and about three inches broad, and on this broad part you may sometimes see one of the gamesters carry the ball tossing it for 40 or 50 yards in spite of all the adverse players; and when he is like to lose it, he generally gives it a great stroke to drive it towards the goal. Sometimes if he miss his blow at the ball, he knocks one of the opposers down: at which no resentment is to be shown. They seldom come off without broken heads or shins in which they glory very much. At this sport one parish sometimes or barony challenges another; they pick out ten, twelve, or twenty players of a side, and the prize is generally a barrel or two of ale, which is brought into the field and drunk off by the victors on the spot, though the vanquished are not without a share of it too. This commonly is upon some very large plain, the barer of grass the better, and the goals are 200 or 300 yards one from the other; and whichever party drives the ball beyond the other's goal wins the day. Their champions are of the younger and most active among them, and their kindred and mistresses are frequently spectators of their address. Two or three bag pipes attend the conquerors at the barrel's head, and then play them out of the field. At some of these meetings two thousand have been present together. They do not play often at football, only in a small territory called Fingal near Dublin the people use it much, and trip, and shoulder very handsomely. These people are reckoned the best wrestlers of the Irish, though I think the best would come off but badly in Moorfields. They have a sort of jargon speech peculiar to themselves, and understand not one word of Irish, and are as little understood by the English. I'll give a sample of it in a lamentation which a mother made over her son's grave, who had been a great fisher and huntsman Ribbeen a Roon, Ribbeen Mourneen, thoo ware good for loand stroand and mounteen, for rig a tool and roast a whiteen, reddy tha taakle gather tha baarnacks drink a grote at nauny hapennys.

The Irish have another custom, to plant an ash or some other tree which will grow big in the middle of the village, though I never observed them to be planters of them anywhere else. In some towns these trees are old and very great, and hither all the people resort with a piper on Sundays or Holydays in the afternoon, where the young folks dance till the cows come home (which by the by they'll do without anyone to drive them). I have seen a short truss young woman tire five lusty fellows, who hereby gets a husband: I am sure I should hardly venture myself with one who had been so able for so many. The elder people sit spectators telling stories of their own like feats in days of yore, and now and then divert themselves with a quill full of sneezing or a [wh]if[f] of tobacco; for one short foul pipe of an inch long, the shorter and fouler the better, will serve a dozen of them men and women together, the first holding the smoke in his mouth until everyone has whiffed once or twice, and when the pipe returns to him he blows it out of his nose. If in the dance the woman be tired, the man throws her to the piper, whose fee is half a penny, and the man if tired is served after the same manner.

Their games within doors are Backgammon and Five Cards, as common here as All Fours in England. They have some superstitious customs among them like ours at All Hallowtide, and observing a hare is an ill omen to a traveller, if it cross his road. I met with an extraordinary piece of superstition in Storye's History of the War of Ireland . . .

You will pardon this tedious digression when I assure it is done with a design to satisfy your curiosity in those things, which though they are used in an island so nearby neighbouring to you, yet perhaps never reached your ears before.

From Naas then after dinner we pursued our voyage, and to the right hand of the town I was shown a house which looks like a little town for bigness. It belonged formerly to one Sir Theophilus Jones, and has a pretty deer-park, but the heir being a minor, I think the place seems a little neglected. When we had rid about a mile on our way we came to a place called Gigginstown, or Strafford's folly; for that great man when he was in the Government here built that house for a country retreat. The length of it is above [blank] yards. It had a chimney for every day of the year, and all the front of it is finely beautified with delicately varigated marble brought from Italy. The rest is of Dutch brick, and though the roof has been down for many years, yet the brick seems as lasting as the marble. It and the spacious gardens show the marks of a very noble design in the master. [blank] miles further is New Bridge, standing on the Liffey, a river rising in the mountains towards the county of Wicklow, and though in any part of its course it is not more than twenty miles from Dublin where it empties itself into the sea, yet from its source to this disemboguement in several meanders it makes a journey of above fourscore miles. It is very well stored with excellent trout, and has several very agreeable seats on its banks, at one of which (that was shown me) called Greenhills sometimes since dwelt the famous Nix, called Swift Nix in England from the robbery he committed near York in the afternoon and came to London, that evening on the same horse. He had a foot company in this Kingdom, and was a man of good substance, but lost all by this last war.

So that what he got over the [blank] back, was lost under his belly. In the evening we came to Balliminnie; it is a small village of poor cabins and an old castle, of which there is abundance in Ireland, built it is said by the Danes, long before the coming of the English into it. They are square strong buildings of stone, with a small door and stone stairs, and windows like spike holes purposely for strength. For as the Danes enlarged their frontiers they built these castles on them as curbs to the neighbouring Irish.

I have often had occasion in some of my letters to mention these cabins or huts but now take the description of them. They build them by putting two forked sticks of such length as they intend the height of the building, and at such distance as they design its length: if they design it longer they place three or four such forks into the ground and on them they lay other long sticks [which are] the ridge timber. Then they raise the wall, which they make of clay and straw tempered with water, and this they call mud: which wall is raised to a sufficient height, which perhaps is four feet. Then they lay other small sticks with one end on the ridge pole and the other on the wall. These they wattle with small hazels, and then cover them with straw or coarse grass, without any chimney, so that when the fire is lighted the smoke will come through the thatch; so that you would think the cabin were on fire. Another sort of their cabins is made by laying one end of the stick upon the bank of a ditch, and the other upon a little bit of a mud wall, and then when it is wattled they cover it with heath, straw, or scraws of earth, and into this miserable place will half a dozen poor creatures creep for shelter and lodging. Their buildings of Versailles are so very magnificent as not capable of such a description that may give a just idea of them; so these in the other extreme are so very wretched things that perhaps the pen of the noblest architect would be very defective in describing them. Behind one of their cabins lies the garden, a piece of ground sometimes of half an acre, and in this is the turf stack, their corn, perhaps two or three hundred sheaves of oats and as much peas. The rest of the ground is full of their dearly beloved potatoes, and a few cabbages which the solitary calf of the family that is here pent from its dam never suffers to come to perfection. I should more exactly have described their dwellings or cabins if I dared have adventured oftener into 'em, or could have stayed in 'em for lice and smoke when I was there.[2] But to proceed in my rambles.

Mrs. Browne invited us, that is Clymene, her husband, and me to her house near adjacent at a place called Morrice farm. She had lived several years in wedlock without ever a child ; they planted an orchard, and the first year it bore any fruit she had a child, and two years after a girl ; they are called Daniel and Hannah, and are the admiration and envy at once of the country. In this town was a wedding of a sculloag's daughter, for so they call their farmers, to another young sculloag. You must note that a man who had six or eight horses and half a dozen cows is reckoned a substantial fellow, and can pay by his ploughing twelve or fourteen pounds rent per annum. Such were the people now to be married, and Mrs. Browne being invited she carried us with her to the house where the kindred of the young folks were all met together, and the priest of the parish, without whom nothing could be done on this occasion. The bride was clad in a red frieze petticoat and waist coat with green tape about the skirts ; on her head she wore a white hood of linen, for they do not wear the kercher until they are married, and she sat in a dark corner of the room with two or three other young women about her. The bridegroom was a strapping young fellow with a grey frieze[3] suit on ; he had brogues on his feet, and [li]ned leather gloves, and a long neck cloth about his neck, as long as any of our steenkirks, and a blue ribbon in his hat. The priest began the ceremony by asking the man, Will you take Nora here present for your lawful wife according to the rites of holy mother church? . . .

Then the bridegroom laid some small pieces of silver for the Arrha, with the ring (which was made of a small twig of an osier handsomely plaited) on the book. Then the priest blessed the ring with two crosses and a short prayer, after which he sprinkled holy water upon it in form of a cross. Then he delivers it to the man, who holding the

---

[2] This description is almost identical with the slightly longer one printed on pp.389-391 of Dunton's *Dublin Scuffle*.
[3] This word was always spelt " frize," as it is still pronounced in Ireland. Cf. description in *London Gazette*, 5 Nov., 1683, of the Brenan brothers who had escaped from Chester Gaol : " They all had on them when they broke prison Irish frize coats with great plate buttons," and *ibidem* No. 1936 re gaol-breaker in a " sad-coloured Kilkenny frize suit."

woman's right hand in his left says, With this ring I thee wed etc., as we do ; then he puts it on the tip of the woman's thumb saying In the name of the father, then on the fore-finger and says Of the son, then on the middle finger saying And of the Holy Ghost, and lastly on the ring finger where he leaves it saying Amen ; and after a few other prayers the business is done. The ring was taken off by one of the young women who I suppose was a sort of bridesmaid, and tied on one of the strings of the bride's purse which hung at her girdle, and it is either worn there or in the bridegroom's hatband until it is either broken or lost. Then liquor went about to all the guests wishing *health, wealth and prosperity* to the young couple. At supper the bride sat at the upper end of the table, and Father James the priest at the right hand. He was a jolly fellow that loved to be much made of, and pretended to be a great traveller ; and many strange things he related to the company that had occurred to his observation abroad. But I found he neither was a tolerable geographer, nor a traveller by any thing but his lies. Here he informed us (and I have had since confirmed by others of good credit) of an ancient custom for the landlord to have the first night's lodging with the maiden bride ; and at this day some of the Earl of Cavan's lands are set with such a clause in the lease. But withal that the bridegroom may buy it off for some small fee, as a hen or a pipe of tobacco.

When jolly Father James got warm, he told us of a young bride . . .

After supper Father James desired to do his last office, which was to bless the genial bed, and accordingly everything being ready, he was carried into a room which was divided by a wattled partition plastered with clay from the room we were in. It had a wattled door which was not impervious to Argus eyes, and made rather to keep out the swine or the calves than for either any privacy or warmth.

He began saying, Our help is in thee, O Lord, who made heaven and earth. The Lord be with you. To which he was answered, And with your spirit. Then he prayed thus, Bless O Lord this bed, that all lying in it may rest in thy peace, and preserve and grow old in observance of thy will, and multiply in length of days, and at last arrive at the Kingdom of Heaven, Amen.

Then he besprinkled it and all the room with holy water which he had brought with him for the nonce; and so his part of the show ended, and exit priest, but not till Clymene, her husband and I had promised to make him a visit the next morning.

I forgot to tell you that after the matrimonial ceremony was over we had a bag piper and a blind harper that dinned us with their music, to which there was perpetual dancing; only whilst we were at supper and blessing the bed. After this ceremony was over it began again, and whilst they were attentive to their sports, Mrs. Bride was vanished, and no news to be heard of her. Her husband seemed vexed at the trick for she was not in the house, but somebody gave him notice where she was (for this was a feint of her modesty), and he found her hid among the cabbages in the garden. When she entered the house all the company descanted on the action and it was generally approved of as an effect of her modesty. We stayed to see them put to bed, but unexpectedly the bride was lost a second time, and no tidings could be had of her, for the mother had conveyed her away so unawares to the company that nobody could tell what became of her. The young fellow sought among the cabbages and potatoes, and all the ditches about the house, but in vain. When he returned he seemed vexed, and told us if we pleased we might see him in bed, but he knew not where his wife was; and so saying he entered his room, and uncased immediately for Bedfordshire where we left him not imagining what could become of the bride. For my part I suspected she had given us the slip to an assignation with the priest or some other lover. But next morning we were informed of the jest, which was the old woman's, her mother's to lock her up in a great wooden chest (which they call a hutch and has an arched cover; it will hold sometimes eight or ten barrels of corn or more) which was in the room. We left them and the family went to their beds, but when Mrs. Bride found her husband began to snore, and took no more notice of her absence, she fell to scratch the boards of the hutch, and knocking with her knuckles and toes. But all in vain, for the husband never wakened, or would not acknowledge it till morning; and she was forced to lie all night in a more uncomfortable place than in the arms of a young bridegroom.

Next morning early without regarding any ceremony we made our visit to Father James, who was just up and wiping his eyes. The weather was very fair, and we stayed at the door (which had a little green field before it) until the room within was swept to receive us. The dew lay in pretty spangles on the grass made by refraction of the sun beams, I had a mind to try the Father's philosophy and enquired what the dew was? He told me it was a vapour that fell upon the ground in the night season, and that the sun drawed it up again in the day ; but Clymene told him it was an old and vulgar notion, and exploded by the newest philosophers, who were of opinion it might be either the moisture which the horses of the sun shake from off their manes when they were put into his chariot rising out of the sea, or that it might be Thetis's chamber maids had emptied Phoebus' pot as soon as he was up, or lastly, and that more probably it was the sweat of the grass and herbs condensed by the cold of the evening air. Her notions made us all laugh, and the priest swore tis gossip by St. Patrick's hand she was as witty as she was pretty, and put some other compliments on her, the best of which were much beneath what she truly deserves. The house was now ready, and the maid came to call us in, where we broke our fast, and prevailed with Father James to accompany us to Kildare, where we were going to be merry. His palfrey was presently saddled and we mounted. We soon came to the Curragh so much noised here. It is a very large plain covered in most places with heath ; it is said to be five and twenty miles round. This is the Newmarket of Ireland, where the horse races are run, and also hunting matches made there being great store of hares, and more game for hawking, all of which are carefully preserved.

They have a tradition (I fancy it was taken from the story of Dido purchasing so much ground as she could surround with ox-hide on which she built Carthage) that St. Bridget the great Saint of Kildare begged from one of the Irish Kings as much land for a common pasture as she could environ with her frieze mantle. The Prince laughed at her, and bade her take it. She cut her mantle into so many small shreds as when tacked together by their ends surrounded all this Curragh or Downs.

Kildare is an ordinary country town not near so good as the Naas, though it gave a name to the county; and is an episcopal see, though but of small revenues, and is now therefore united to the deanery of Christchurch which is the King's Royal Chapel in Dublin, as the Bishopric of Rochester is to the deanery of Westminster in England. It has in it the Cathedral church with two or three inns, and those very sorry ones. It has two fairs yearly and a weekly market, and sends two burgesses to the parliament. After all it is but a poor place, not lying in any road, and not having any trade belonging to it. There are some shops with hops, iron, salt and tobacco, and the merchant not worth forty pound. This county gives the title of Earl to one of the family of the Fitzgeralds, formerly called Geraldines, who came over into Ireland among the first adventurers in Henry II's reign, and is now first Earl here as Oxford is with you. Here we dined on a dish of large trouts, and with some bottles of wine made ourselves merry. When we took horse our Landlord told us we must accept of a Deoch a' dorais from him, which is a drink at the door. He had a bottle of brandy under his arm and a little wooden cup with which he presented each of us a dram. From whence we went about two miles backwards towards the King's County to view the Earl of Kildare's chair. It is an old castle built on the side of a hill, which overlooks all the neighbouring country. I was told it was built by some of the Earls of Kildare as a watch tower, for which purpose it was very well placed.

From hence we had a lovely prospect towards the north of a noble vale, part of which was covered with corn and part with cattle, with some woods, among which were seen some houses of good bulk and show raising their heads. Beyond these were hills on which stood several great houses; a fine river ran through the valley; on another side the greatest part of the Curragh lay open to our view, which indeed is a noble plain.

After we had satisfied our eyes with staring about we steered our course towards the Bog of Allen which though it be the greatest in Ireland, yet never was so famous as in the last rebellion, where the Rapparees had their rendezvous when they designed any mischief on the country, to the number of five or six hundred, and where they easily hid themselves when pursued. For, as I am informed, this bog is near fifty miles long, with many woods in it, and some islands of very good and profitable land, as the Island of Allen which they say is worth eight hundred pounds per annum.

Since I have named the Rapparees, I think it will not be improper to tell you something of them, because it relates a little to the ancient warfare of the Irish. In this war I think they were first called Rapparees. They were some loose and undisciplined people who were not subject to command, but like freebooters made everything that belonged to the English a prey if they could come at it. Their arms, like those of the old Irish Kearns were a half pike and a skeane. They made their excursions generally in the night, or by surprise, lying in ambuscade for their prey, which they had a true and constant intelligence of from the other Irish who seemed laborious people all day, but at night were as great rogues as the best of them. At length they got fire arms and ammunition, but never any courage, so that a party of the English militia of forty or fifty men would willingly engage two hundred of them, but they could never be prevailed with to stand. You may judge by this story what martial men these untrained Rapparees are. For a lusty fellow in the late King's reign was taken into the regiment of guards for a musketeer, and being at exercise in the field where they discharged their pieces to accustom them to firing, one man's gun did not go off at the first fire. However, he charged a second time with the rest of his rank. It also missed the second time, and he put in his third bandolier of powder, and then it went off with such a recoil as stunned the fellow. So that he let the gun fall out of his hand; the serjeant ran and took it up, but the soldier called out to him saying: Serjeant Joy take care of what you do, for by my soul, I put three the full of the bandolier in, and there is but one gone out yet. The ancient division of the Irish soldiery was into the Kearns, which were such as these Rapparees, and their Galloglasses. These were composed of their better sort of men, who fought on horseback with poleaxes. They were called Galloglasses from the words 'Gall,' white or neat, and 'Oglach,' young men. But those who composed their armies in the late troubles were exercised and trained after the common way of other soldiers. From hence we returned to Ballimennie after we had left Father James at home.

His majesty for encouragement to breed large and serviceable horses in this kingdom has been pleased to give a hundred pounds per annum out of his treasury here to buy a plate, which they run for at the Curragh in September. The horses that run are to carry twelve stone each, and therefore there are several fine horses kept hereabouts for the race in stables built on purpose. There is another race yearly run here in March or April for a plate of a hundred guineas, which are advanced by the subscription of several gentlemen. The course is four measured miles and is run [*blank*] Thursday the 13th. of September was the day of the race this year for the King's Plate. There was a vast concourse of people to see it from all parts of the kingdom. My Lord Galway (one of the Lords Justices) was present at the race, and other persons of great quality. I met in the Curragh (when the race was run) with my worthy friend Mr. Searl, whose character you have in my Dublin Journal and several others that I know in Dublin. After the race was over our company rid to Ballimany.[5] At this village is a little thatched house like one of our English country houses, built by the Earl of Meath. After we had seen all the rooms in this nobleman's thatched house (which I design to describe in my Summer Ramble) we left Ballimany, and dined that day at the Naas, and reached Dublin about 9 in the evening.

Letter No. 5

My mind is always with you and my dear friends in England, though at present I am in the country of wrath and vengeance if the Etymon of Ireland be true ; and though you may fancy that little diversion can be received from an account of a place of which you may have formed some disadvantageous prejudices, yet remember that without the assistance of filth and ordure the sweetest flowers and fairest fruits are often lost, and though it undeservedly be called the Land of Ire on one side, and Insula Sanctorum or Island of Saints on the other,

---

[5] Dunton spells this place-name in three different ways in one letter, which is typical of the casualness of the period in this respect.

I cannot assent to its deserving either, because I find a mean which forbids one and denies the other.

When I came to Dublin I took up my lodging at the house of one Polydore in Wine-Tavern Street, who with his wife Glaucopia gave me very civil entertainment. Polydore is a man of good acquaintance in this town, and his profession of the law and business in the courts makes him generally known, and to him I am obliged for much of my conversation here ; his Glaucopia is a person so fair, and of so sweet a mien and conversation, as makes her not only the comfort of her husband's life, but the delight of all that know her.

'Twas with them I began the sally upon my first Ramble to Malahide to eat oysters, where they may be dredged out of the sea almost at any time. But before I proceed on my journey give me leave to make you some short descriptions of the company that went with us. Don Quixote was Ephipia's husband, one who for want of better performances, was obliged to all the obsequious observances that a coquette wife could expect, when he married her his circumstances were low, and had been such a sufferer by both the poxes, that the one had disfigured his face, and curing the other had emaciated his body, and you'll say with me that such an one might very well endeavour with meal to compensate for the deficiencies of his malt. He was clad in such a dress as bespoke his desire of living to be old ; his wig was of the most fashionable size, and surely if the wigs now in mode were ever useful to anyone they are for such, whose heads require much warmth, and faces something to hide them. The palfrey he was mounted on was worthy of such a wight, as lean as himeslf, he had been an hunter and of good shapes, but being strained beyond his ability he had broken his wind, or else he had hardly left a better master to come into his hands, whom he carried with a Mountera cap, and a pair of rusty pistols, with a borrowed blue cloak ; I am sure I should prefer the happy state of Lucian's ass, to the Rosinante thus charged.

With us went two coaches, in one of which sate Ephipia his wife ; she had been a saddler's widow, who being a man of wealth (as trading people are here counted if worth a thousand pounds) and charged but with one daughter.

She had not been long in that state, 'ere a thousand flies came buzzing about her honeypot, and I fancy the main motive that prevailed upon her to accept of her Quixote was (as they say) to give the knave a kiss to be quit of him, for she like other wise widows never let him be master of all, that he might be always subject to her, as he gave her sufficient demonstration by his assiduity at the coach door, even to advising her to put on her mask to preserve the dear face from cold.

Senecis was an old bachelor, and had paid for his celibacy, as well by the last poll-tax as by the distempers which brought him under the surgeon's hands, one who pretended great regards for the fair sex, but admired how men that gave themselves any time to think should ever fall in love, for which reason we placed him near the fair and ingenious Clymene, whose black eyes, and hair, and skin truly fair, and her more beautiful mind, had fortune been kind, would have advanced her to a more agreeable husband than Cursorio, for beside the external graces she was adorned with, she had a soul with all the meekness of a martyr and vivacity of an amorous poet.

Two more whose names I forget were with us but they shewed so cold an indifference towards one another as would have made any man judge them man and wife, long under the conjugal yoke.

A rambling bookseller was among the company, one that by his whimsical journeys and the merriment of his behaviour, seeming void of all care, you would guess were a beggar, and by his reading good books before he sold them, and the just application of his learned acquisitions to the several actions of his life, he seemed an honest man raised upon good foundations, and one good quality more he had (pardon my lavishness in a bookseller's praise) that he was a true lover of his friend, and very ready to give more satisfactory assurances than the common professors of that noble passion will trouble themselves with.

The last of our company was a young Scotch gentleman who was a lieutenant in the army, and by his courteous behaviour seemed well-natured and brave.

Thus accompanied we took coach and the first thing I shall take notice of at our going out of town was the house in which the Lord Chancellor of this kingdom dwells. It is an handsome large house of four rooms on a floor, the front covered with jessamine up to the easings of the house, and some lime trees planted before it; next to this stands another large building belonging to one Alder. Piercy of this city, it is designed for the next year's Lord Mayor to keep his mayoralty in. This Alderman Piercy is a very rich man and of a fair character, he is the son of the Piercy who made such a bustle in London about proving himself heir to the ancient earls of Northumberland, but being found an impostor was finally obliged to stand in the courts at Westminster Hall with a paper fixed on his breast setting forth his crime: but here they say his misfortunes had raised too powerful pretenders to that estate against him who baffled his right, but whatever it was the Alderman has raised his own fortunes by his own industry, to such an height, as he never needs think of his father's pretentions, nor envy those who enjoy them. A little beyond this place is the strand where every evening the gentry in their coaches or on horseback make their tours as you do in Hyde Park. Hence we saw Ring's End which is compared to a neck of mutton in breadth, because it lies in the sea environed by its waters, and is a long straggling village. Most of our way to Malahide we kept near the sea, and on the left we were diverted with the agreeable prospect of several good houses and a fine grove called Clontarf Wood, a place where men of heat go to bleed one another in duels, and those possessed with the gentler fire of love carry their mistresses to take the country air, and find their names growing on the trees. We met with the skeleton of a church, which was gone to decay since the spirit that possessed it was fled, I mean the revenue that belonged to it being translated to a neighbouring one more convenient for the inhabitants. Next to this we came through a little Irish town of about nine cabins with two chimneys each, at one end one, and the doors were placed all in the back part of the house, a thing not very usual in England. But leaving this contemptible habitation we came to such another little place, and about 2 miles farther the town of Malahide saluted our eyes with the best figure it could make, because the nearer we approached it the worse it appeared. In Dublin there is a saying about it, that

If you go to Malahide
carry your bottle by your side.

I suppose the reason is because it is so hard to get drink there. It contains about thirty ordinary huts in all, and not one without several little children who were sprawling about the fireplace (for there was but small appearance of fire on it) like so many maggots on a dunghill in a summer's day. One Jones's house was the Inn and that but a poor ordinary place: they have no bogs hereabouts, to cut turf or peat in, and therefore the poor people such as dwell in this town are hardly put to it for firing, for English coal is too dear, and that they must bring from Dublin, so that they are forced to burn straw or furzes, whence arose the saying that, In Fingall when the wisp's out, the fires out all. When we came to alight at the Inn where our Don Quixote rode before to provide for Ephipia's reception with the rest of our company, the coach in which she was not being come up he mounted Rosinante in haste, and scoured back to see what was become of her, but the coach met him before he went far, and Clymene handsomely rallied him for his assiduity about his wife, saying, men whiles courting are our most humble fawning slaves until they acquire their aims, and then become as tyrannical in their indifference towards us as they were submissive and cringing before, but you Quixote betray the rights your sex has so long been possessed of when once they get us into their clutches. Ephipia appeared nettled at her words, but obeisant husband seemed very well pleased that he was taken notice of for it. One Father Gowan or Smith as he called himself, à la mode de Angleterre, happened to be in the Inn at our arrival, where hearing he was priest of the parish, I engaged his company with us at dinner for I had never seen any of their clergy before. He was a jovial sort of a fellow and looking upon us as a parcel of citz that had more money than wit, he was not sparing of his own as often as he had any opportunity given him to shew it; and had it not been for him we had been baulked in getting any oysters, the main end of our journey, for it was Easter Monday and observed among them as a great holiday. Not one could be prevailed on to get any though for hire; but he had a power over them which procured us some, such is the authority these priests usurp over their besotted laity, that an obedience to them is looked upon as an action highly meritorious, which the priest confirmed by this argument upon my taking notice of the absolute power I saw he had over them, for said he, if they are obliged to observe the dictates of heaven, then surely they must observe those of heaven's ministers, but the antecedent is true and therefore the consequence. We were all surprised at the impudence of the man to syllogize that way upon a company of strangers and so fallaciously too, but in hopes by approving of him, he might make us more diversion I told him that such men of learning as he, might easily enforce anything upon us by his arguments, and therefore we acquiesced in what he said; he seemed to divine what I told him, but withal let us know he had learnt his course of philosophy before he was sixteen years old, but that since being taken up with the care of souls he had mightily forgotten it.

Dinner now came in, we had salt fish and eggs, hen and bacon, and rabbits, but our liquor was very ordinary; one thing I observed here, which was that when the woman of the house or her maid brought a quart of ale to us she poured some into the glass and drank it off. I enquired the cause of that custom, and Father Smith informed us, it was to take away any suspicion of poison being in the liquor, that they perform that office of a taster for their guests.

After dinner it was proposed for merriment that every man should tell his tale; and we that were English told each his story and some of them satirical enough upon our own countrymen, and then Father Smith began with his to this purpose, that after a sermon where the advantages and necessity of auricular confession had been fully shown, a man and his wife going home talked of the sermon and seeing confession was so necessary a thing they thought themselves obliged to it, but believed it more prudent that they should confess their sins to one the other than to strangers; thus then they agreed that at home they should fall to the observing the directions of the sermon; accordingly, when evening came, and the hearth was cleaned with a good fire in the chimney, and a jug of ale by their sides, the good man and his wife fell to the directed exercise; after some dispute who should begin it fell to the wife, who desired him to forgive the faults she had committed, and that she would not conceal the least she could remember; she then began and told him she had a trick to steal malt out of the hutch, and wheat sometimes, and now and then a fleece of wool, all which she converted into money to make merry with her friends and neighbours, and that sometimes when he came home fuddled she used to steal out of his pockets some of his small money which she applied to the same uses with the other goods; for all which she heartily begged his pardon and promised to do so no more. The husband freely forgave all, and told her those things were hers as well as his and therefore the crime was not so great as she might think, but says he, have you been always true to my bed? This made her blush, and ask him could he forgive her? He answered it was for that end they did confess, and he was resolved to forgive all, then saith she, it was once my misfortune to violate your bed though indeed and indeed I could not help it, for last harvest was twelve month, let me see, yes it was then, and a very hot day when all the servants were abroad at work in reaping wheat. I only was left in the house, where overcome with the fatigue of getting victuals ready for the labourers, and the heat of the day I laid me down and fell asleep on the green rushes on the floor, when your servant Hugh, ay, it was that rogue, I shall never forget him, came in to carry out some drink to the field, and finding me in that posture and overcome with weariness and sleep, committed that base thing upon me before I was well awake; indeed I knew it was in vain to call for help, and I was not able to make any resistance, I thought to acquaint you with it, but then I feared your resentments and so concealed it until now, for which I heartily ask your forgiveness, that being the only time of my transgression. The good man took her in his arms and embracing her told [her] it was a great sin, but he prayed God to forgive her, as he did, and so all was well. And then he began his part which was that he used to lessen to her the price of the goods which he sold at the market to answer some of his private expenses, and that was all he was guilty of; but quoth she, have you not done the thing with anybody else since you were my husband? To which he desired her to remember the freedom that he used in passing by her fault, and prayed her to follow the example he had set her. Well says she, let me hear the circumstances of your crime before I give my judgment; he then told her that when their last little boy was christened she might remember how he was fuddled in entertaining his gossips and friends at the christening, and that night when the company was gone he had committed the fault with their maid Sheila, for which he begged God and her to forgive him. To which she said Amen because he was then overcome with drink, and she herself not fit for his use. But is this all, did you never do it but that once? Yes saith he, once more when you were violently troubled with the toothache, and being unwilling to disturb you I applied myself to Sheila again who was as condescending as before. The wife hereat all enraged flung the jug at his head calling him a damned rogue, and wishing he might never be forgiven in heaven any more than she would forgive it here, for you base fellow, said she, could you think that any pain, though greater than the toothache, could make me an unfit match for you. At this the company laughed heartily, the women hung their heads and seemed abashed, though one might easily perceive they approved of the wife's action.—Senecio here fell abawling against this inconvenience of matrimony, that when the woman was not in a condition to be a fit and meet help to her husband, he must still wait her time, without using such means as nature and celibacy would have allowed to ease himself of his trouble, he said a great deal more but because it carried him into some smuttiness not fit for the women's ears we desired him to hold and let the lieutenant begin his tale which he did thus.

Gentlemen you have been all very free with your own countrymen, and I shall follow your example and for your diversion take the same liberty with mine. . . .

The story made us all laugh as the most satirical we had ever heard, and the priest's manner of expressing his contempt for the Scotch king made us laugh a great deal more. After this the women took their turns to divert us with their voices, and indeed it was better performed by everyone of them than I expected, even our landlady was brought in to sing an Irish Cronaan, which is so odd a thing that I cannot express it, being mostly performed in the throat only now and then some miserable sounds are sent through the nose. After this it came into my head to put a casuistical question to Father Smith to hear his solution which with the leave and permission of the company I did thus . . .

It was now near time to return home, and having paid our reckoning we took coach and came back a different way from that we went, where we found a place called the Warren House, because it stands near a warren of rabbits. Here we met with an Irish girl with hair and eyes black as sloe, ruddy cheeks and a very white skin, the company considered her as a very agreeable and charming piece of flesh and for my part I thought I had never seen anything more pleasing. You will not wonder I was so much surprised with this Irish woman when I tell you black is a colour I have always loved and admired to such a degree, that I much preferred the Black Raven for a sign to anything of another colour, and Cowley who was the English Ovid handsomely tells us if she be black what lover loves not night. I fancied the rustic dress she wore of coarse linen and ordinary frieze, was a great addition to her unadulterated charms, which I had no sooner communicated to the company than Clymene took her aside and changed dresses with her. The metamorphosis was surprising to us all, Clymene in the country dress looked like one bewitched and the other lost all the sweet and native innocence which she wore in her looks, each behaving themselves very unnaturally to the garb they wore, so that we all agreed that particular faces and persons had dresses peculiar to set them off to advantage. Though I left the charming rustic behind me, her idea shall remain lively in my breast. Between this and Dublin we met not anything remarkable saving a lapwing's nest which Polydore deprived of its eggs. This is the bird that according to the poets wears the mask of Terence's unfortunate cruelty, it has a little crest of feathers on its head the semblance of his crown, and under its tail we could see red feathers, the bloody marks of what he had committed upon Philomena. Thus far the poets, but the description of the naturalists is delivered by Mr. Willoughby in his History of Birds; the eggs were of a dirty colour speckled with black spots. The lapwing is also called the Tewit, I suppose from its cry, and is kept in gardens to devour the insects. As we came near the shore we saw a cormorant swimming on the water. It was the first I had ever seen, and inquiring of a naturalist in Dublin about the vulgar received opinion that it has but one gut, he assured me that on his dissecting one he found it had a stomach, but not like granivorous birds, and several guts which are very small, in which were contained several bones of fish. It is near as big as a goose, and of almost a black colour, the breast is grey, and has a neck and bill like that of a goose. This gentleman told me that in some parts of England (as well as China where 'tis frequently done) they fish with these birds after they are tamed, and manned as hawks are. They carry them abroad hooded, and tie a string about their necks so as to contract their gullet that they cannot swallow the fish, and when they come to the place they let them go, and when they dive and bring up any game they fly to hand, and answering their keeper's call come to him with the fish in their mouth, which is only bruised with their bill, and then betake themselves to the water again. When they have done the master rewards them with some o' the fish; one thing that is said of them is very strange, viz., that though they be flatfooted like duck and geese, yet they often perch upon trees and build their nests in 'em. Soon after we arrived at Dublin, where we all separated to our respective homes

I had no sooner done ruminating on my Malahide Ramble, and put my observations into the order I have here presented you with, than another vagary took me to make a small excursion towards Drogheda, pursuant to which I equipped me with all necessaries for the journey. It happened to be upon Saturday in Easter week, that I set forth about ten of the clock well mounted, and provided for the new discoveries I was upon. Drumcondra was the first town I passed through, after I left the strand; it has a couple of good houses in it, besides several others for dairy folks and tipplers; the master of the place is one Sir John Coghill, judge of the Prerogative Court, and one of the Masters of Chancery; two miles further is Santry, the seat of the Barrys, Lords Barons of Santry; the grandfather of the present lord, who is a minor, was Lord Chief Justice of the King's Bench in Ireland, and one who by his great knowledge in the laws, and undaunted resolution in seeing them justly executed where it fell under his province, did acquire a considerable estate, and greater reputation, and was the first nobleman of the family. The mansion house is not very considerable, but the gardens and orchards take up near thirty acres of land. A little beyond this place I was overtaken by a couple of people, man and wife upon one horse, they were clad after the Irish manner, but I could not imagine of what country they were by the gibberish they spoke, and the woman's sitting on horseback with her face the wrong way ; they were mounted on a little well-set ambling hobby which went at a swift rate. I set spurs to my steed to keep up with them and enquired what country they were of ; they spoke several words to me, but none that I understood save Fingal, which put me in mind of the gibberish used in that territory, and made me know they were Fingallians. The fellow was a crafty knave and though at first he spoke in that unintelligible cant, he came to be better natured and speak tolerable English and was my companion almost to Drogheda. Three miles from Santry is the town called Swords, a pretty large town consisting most of Irish houses, though there be three or four good ones, one of which is an inn and tavern ; here they have a very mournful song in memory of one Tom Taylor, who was I think landlord of the town and a fine sort of fellow among them, could I express it to you as comically as it was sung to me I had certainly sent it to you, for you know action is so much the life of many things, that without it they are not only dull but senseless too. Four miles farther is Ballough, a poor sorry town with an inn where the stage-coach to Drogheda sets in at noon ; two miles further is Balruddery, they told me it was the place where travellers between Drogheda and Dublin usually refreshed themselves in a very good inn which was then there ; but by an unfortunate and rare accident the reputation of the town was utterly lost a little before the restoration of Charles 2nd. Some travellers happened to lie at the best inn, when they went away no one could tell. In some time they were wanting, and no news could be had of them, this was the last place they were seen in, and therefore an account was to be expected of them here, but none to be had, innkeeper with his servants and some other people of the town were secured, though all denied having any knowledge of them, but a smith confessed he was employed by the master of the inn with some others to knock out their brains, and those of their horses with his hammer ; upon this eleven of them were committed to jail, and soon after arraigned and tried ; the smith said the horses were buried in one place, and the men in another, but on search there were no such things found, nor any marks of the grounds being lately stirred; however at the trial the smith confessed the fact and pleaded guilty; and accused all the rest as having an hand in it. Now murder in Ireland is treason, by statute, and consequently all are principals who are concerned in it, on which the jury found 'em guilty. By the way let me tell you the lost persons, the criminals, the judges, sheriff and jury were all protestants, and so no foul play was supposed to be done them, but they were convicts by the sole accusation of the smith, an English protestant. In short they were all carried to execution, the smith was hanged confessing and confirming all he had said before, and seeming very penitent. Some of the others died as positively denying what the smith had declared, and appealed to God to witness the truth of what they said. This much surprised the sheriff, who knew them to be protestants and not subject to equivocation. He ordered some of the next that were hanged up to be immediately cut down, and when they came to themselves persuaded them that [the] rope accidentally broke, and gave them hopes of a reprieve for some time if they would confess, but they still asserted their innocence, and were trussed up a second time, and thus they all finished their days, and nothing was ever heard since then of the lost persons. So here you have an unaccountable testimony of one man though with the loss of his own life against ten other persons who died with all the solemn denials of fact. Five miles hence is Gormanstown, the seat of the Prestons lords viscounts of Gormanstown. Not far from hence is the fatal place where one of those lords in the horrid Rebellion of '41 betrayed Major Roper with 600 English, who were marching to Drogheda, and all slain by a party of the Irish, for this lord had retarded their march and entertained the officers at his house until the enemy had notice, and laid an ambush for them.

Drogheda lies upon the Boyne, which runs through it, within three miles of the sea. It is a large walled town but not able to make any defence against the attacks now used, though Cromwell lost a good many men in taking it, but all the world knows how much the art of war is since improved. Here is a large church and house belonging to the Primate of all Ireland; it has a tholsell and custom-house over which the collector is the chief officer. It is governed by a mayor, two sheriffs and aldermen, and they have a custom that as soon as ever their mayor is sworn on Michaelmas-day in the morning an account of it is sent by an express to Dublin, which in four hours or less conveys it thither, though I could never learn the origin of it, yet they say here that the Lord Mayor of Dublin is not to be sworn until he hears the Mayor of Drogheda is. In short it is an handsome clean English-like town, and the best that I have seen in Ireland except the metropolis; about three little miles to the Northwest up the river is Oldbridge, the place where the battle of the Boyne was fought, when I was on the spot where great Schomberg fell I could not consider it without some melancholy reflections on humanity, that he who was so famous a general and had made so much noise in the world by his conduct and successes in many great actions should fall in a place where no trophy, no monument is erected to his name, more than what he himself had purchased by his great deeds, and this last generous engagement of the enemy at the head of a few men whom he led through the river. The country hereabouts is very pleasant and fertile and very well worth contending for, but before I leave the Boyne I shall take notice to you of one thing peculiar to this river, that is the salmon in it are always fat and never out of season, which is a rarity not to be met with in England that ever I heard. I shall also crave your leave to tell you that in the new edition of Camden's Britannia page 998 where the course of the Boyne is described, Athboy among other towns is placed upon it, whereas the Boyne runs through Trim, and Athboy is five miles beyond it, so you see that the best geographical accounts may fail in their exactness without an autopsy. I got home to Dublin safe enough, having a proverb on my side, etc. [Nothing is omitted here: the letter ends thus abruptly.]

Letter No. 6

'Tis not long since I had done sowing my wild oats, and now I am earnestly hunting after gapeseed, you should smile if you have the picture of your quondam friend at the Black Raven, like an overgrown oak newly come to town staring and gazing at all the signs and everything else in the streets pacing out their length, and inquiring ever and anon, what call you this street, who dwells in yon great house, whose fine coach is that? For thus I rambled through every street, alley and corner of this spacious town, which though it be twelve times less than London, is yet the biggest next to it in all our dominions.

I do not trouble you with the account of its original or antiquity since Mr. Camden (out of whom the Exact Description of Ireland is taken) has given so short and full relation of it, and the situation ; but content myself to begin at Ring's-End the place of my landing. When the tide is in, 'tis a peninsula having but one avenue to it by land from the south, tis a small village with three or four tolerable brick houses covered with tile or slates, besides several other less ones ; it has no shelter, nor gardens and consequently a very bleak place, exposed to all winds and weather ; upon the highest part of this neck of land is a gibbet lately set up on which hangs one they say was called Abraham De Grove a German doctor. His crime was extraordinary and therefore worth acquainting you with it ; he had been some months in Dublin, and one day met with a Dutchman, master of a ship who was of his former acquaintance, him he [carried] to a tavern, and from thence home with him to his lodging, where after some supper and wine below stairs, with his landlady, and a Dutch shoemaker of the neighbourhood, he carried the skipper to his chamber. Next day the doctor kept his room until night, and had all day an unusual fire in it and some vessels of water brought him by the maid which he received at the door pretending to be at some chemical operation ; she asked him where was the Dutchman and he told her he went out about six in the morning, to make which story likely the doctor himself went to the street door before the family was stirring and opened it for it was only bolted. When night came he borrowed his landlord's cloak, or wide coat, to go abroad in for fear of cold, and returned twice to his lodging before bedtime. In fine the thing was thus, he murdered the skipper the night before, and in the great fire burnt all his clothes, and head, and one arm which had a Jerusalem mark on it. The next day a new castor was found in a waste piece of ground in Dames Street, and the trunk and legs of a man separated one from the other on the river side, where the tide had left them. The Dutch crew wanting their master were alarmed at this, and coming among the rest to see the limbs knew one of the legs by marks of a shot on it, hence they went among his acquaintance and traced him to this barbarian's lodging, who could give no account of him, but on searching his room the skipper's shoebuckles, tweezers, waistcoat buttons, and several other little things all of silver were found hid in several parts of the chamber, the sides of the bedstead were all bloody, some of the blood found mixed with lime in a trunk, and one or two teeth among the ashes unburnt, as also a piece of his coat and some ha[ir], notwithstanding all this and great quantities of clotted blood in the privy, this wretch denied all with an unusual impudence at his trial, feasted himself after condemnation in the jail, was deaf to all the clergy's endeavours to make him confess saying it was against law to execute a man without confession (for so it is in Germany) and died obstinate and hard.

After some refreshment here I looked towards Dublin but how to come at it I no more knew than the fox at the grapes, for though I saw a large strand yet twas not to be walked over because of a pretty rapid stream which must be crossed. I enquired for a coach, but found no such thing was to be had here unless by accident ; but was informed that I might have a Ring's End car, which upon my desire was [got] and I got upon it, not into it. It is a perfect car with two wheels and towards the back of it a seat is raised crossways, long enough to hold three people, the cushion mine had was made of patchwork but of such coarse kind of stuff that I fancied they had stolen some poor beggar's coat for a covering, between me and the horse upon the cross bars of the car stood my charioteer who presently set his horse into a gallop which so jolted our sides though upon a smooth strand that I was in purgatory until I got at Lazy-hill, where I paid three halfpence for my fare of half a mile's riding, and almost as pleased as the young gentleman that drove the chariot of the sun would have been, to be rid of my seat. However they are a great conveniency and you may go to Ring's End from Dublin, or from hence thither with a load of goods for three pence or a groat, and I was told there are one hundred more plying hereabouts that you can hardly be **disappointed**.

Lazy or Lacy's Hill is a suburb of Dublin in which are very good houses, here dwell anchor-smiths, and stand two glass houses, though n[one] of them were at work by reason of the scarcity of coals ; the glasses made here and at another in the northern suburb are very fine and clear, and not a very great price, a flint glass of about a pint and half being sold for eight or nine pence.

Between this place and the city stands Trinity College, the sole University of Ireland, an account of which I now give you not as the observation of my first day's landing, but as what I have since seen and informed myself of. It consists of three squares, the outward being as large as both the inner, one of which of modern building has not chambers on every side, the other has ; on the south side of which stands the library, the whole length of the square well furnished with choice books, a great part of which were the library of the famous Bishop the Primate of Armagh, who I am assured was the first scholar that ever entered in this house and the first who took degrees in it ; in the south west end of which is an handsome new skeleton of a man, made up and given by Dr. Gwither a physician of careful and happy [memory], of great integrity, learning and sound judgement, as may be seen by those treatises of his that are inserted in some late Philosophical Transactions ; at the east end on the right hand is a chamber called the Countess of Bath's Library, filled with many handsome folios and other books in Dutch binding gilt, with the earl's arms impressed upon them for he had been sometimes of this house ; on the left hand opposite to this room another chamber in which are contained a great many manuscripts, medals and other curiosities. The hall and butteries run the same range with the library, and separate the two inner squares ; it is an old building, as also the Regent house, which from a gallery looks into the chapel, which has been of late years enlarged, being before too little for the number of [   ] which are now with the fellows and masters, reckoned about 340. They have a garden for the fellows, and another for the Provost, both neatly kept, as also a bowling-green and large parks for the students to walk and exercise in. The foundation consists of a Provost (who at present is the Reverend Dr. George Brown, a gentleman bred in this house since a youth when he was first entered, and one in whom they all count themselves very happy as an excellent governor) seven senior fellows of whom two are Doctors in Divinity, eight junior to which one is lately added by .... and seventy scholars, their public commencements are at shrovetide and the first Tuesday after the eight . . . .[1] Their Chancellor is his Grace the Duke of Ormond. Since the death of the right reverend the late Bishop of Meath they have had no Vice-Chancellor only *pro re nata*. The University was founded by Queen Elizabeth and by her and her successors largely endowed and many munificent gifts and legacies since made by several other well disposed persons, all whose names, together with their gifts are read publicly in the chapel every Trinity Sunday in the afternoon, as a grateful acknowledgement to the memory of their Benefactors. About three years ago they celebrated their first secular day, when the Provost Dr. Ash, now Bishop of Clogher, preached and made an handsome entertainment for several persons of quality, *on the 9th of January 1693 which completed a century from the foundation of the college.*[2] Its arms are [*blank.*]

To the front of the college is a large and spacious street called College Green, on the north side of which is the Parliament House formerly called Chichester House, as belonging to the Chichester Earls of Donegal, and either purchased or hired by King Charles the Second for this use, it is an old building and has little remarkable in it, but the two houses, the Conference chamber and other rooms are all conveniently placed, with a piece of ground that was formerly a garden and serves now for a place to walk in, to the south of this street stands a building like an oven of an oval figure, which has been taken by other strangers as well as myself for a town oven, but it is a church named from Saint Andrew, and though it make no great shew of bigness, it doth in its galleries and pews contain a greater number of people than its outside appearance would make one think.

I cannot make any judgement of the figure of the city because the walls are covered with houses so that one cannot well surround them. It has seven gates (though in Mr. Camden's time, and in Mr. Eachard's Exact Description it

---
[1] The edge of the paper of the original MS. is cut off at this point and several words are partly missing.
[2] The words in italics have been added to the MS. in another hand, as have some minor corrections here and there which I have ignored.

has but six), viz., Dames Gate, Warbroughs, Pauls, Newgate, Ormond Gate, Bridge Gate and Essex Gate. I confess this last was built long since Camden's days but the exact describer came long after its building. I know nothing more that is remarkable in this part of the suburb.

To the northward of this nearer to the city lie the Council Chamber and Custom house, of both which I shall speak in due time. I had now taken up lodging in Wine-Tavern Street, and the first jaunt I took was at ten of the clock to Christ Church, where the bell rang to prayers. It is a large handsome pile, well beautified within side, and has a very good organ which I am told cost £1500. Hither the government come to church as the King's Chapel Royal, they sit over the Great Door of the choir and the ascent to it from the aisle is by two large staircases, all the other things are such as we see in our cathedrals. To the north of the choir is a place called St. Mary's Chapel, what it formerly was I cannot tell, but at present there is nothing in it but some tombstones.

In the middle of the great aisle on the south side by the wall is to be seen the tomb of Richard Strongbow, earl of Pembroke, the first English adventurer in the conquest of Ireland, he has the effigies of half his son lying by him, whom they say he cut into two at the middle for showing some fear in an engagement with the Irish. In the wall above are these words inscribed in gilded letters: This ancient monument of Richard Strongbow called Comes Stranguliae Lord of Chepstow and Ogny the first and principal invader of Ireland 1169, the monument was broken by the fall of the roof and body of Christ Church in anno 1567, and set up again at the charges of the Right Honourable Sir Henry Sydney, knight of the noble Order Lord President of Wales, Lord Deputy of Ireland 1570.

The bells of this church are six, and go the chimes at the hours of four, eight and twelve to the tune of a psalm. This church is governed by a dean, who is the present Bishop of Kildare, a chancellor, and seven prebendaries, the verger walks before the dean into church, with a silver rod in his hand, and divine service is performed here three times every day except Sundays and holy days (viz.) at six in the morning, ten, and four in the afternoon. And one thing I have observed very commendable here, that a man may spend nine hours every day in public prayers at the several churches, and the holy sacrament is administered in some one of them every Sunday in the year; and though this pious observation of public service be a thing highly commendable, yet there is another custom used in this church to the great scandal of it in the eyes of all sober people, and that is whilst divine worship is performing or the preacher in the pulpit in the choir, you shall see all sorts of men walking in the aisles, and men of business make it too often their Sunday exchange. I could not without amazement see some rustling powdered beaus, swearing with as little concern as in a coffee house, and their talk much the same the last night's debauch, or lewdness, as if commital of them were not sufficient provocation to pull vengeance on their heads, without the extravagant impudence, as it were to nose the Almighty with the repetition of them in the place appointed for His worship, for their devotion is only to the music, and the ladies. The steeple of this church is square and has a dial on every side.

Near this is the Tholsell or exchange. It is a small building, square, neat enough, but scarce big enough for the company that comes on it at high change, which is at half an hour after twelve, it has two fronts, one southward, and the other westward, upon three arches each, there is an ascent to it by large stone stairs between the pillars of the arches of square stone, it is railed, and iron spikes on the top. Over the change are the room where the Lord Mayor and Aldermen meet upon business or at feasts, and another where the sheriffs and commons sit, their floors are supported by four strong stone pillars. Over the entrance at the west front is a large balcony supported by two pillars of stone, and above the balcony in notches stand stone statues of the 2 Charles in their robes bigger than the life. In the eastern part of the Exchange is a small square place where the Sessions of the city and its other courts are held. On top or pinnacle of the building is a globe and on that a weathercock gilded. And now I am speaking of this public place, give me leave to say something of the present Government of it. The Companies that belong to it are two or three and twenty, they are governed by a lord Mayor, 24 aldermen, two sheriffs and a common council until the year 'sixty-six or 'sixty-seven, they were never called other than Mr. Mayors, and have now such Ensigns of honour as a sword, cap of maintenance, etc., as the Lord Mayor of London, for so we imitate things above us. They have a Recorder, and five Justices of the Peace, all aldermen ; they hold quarterly Sessions, and try people for their lives. It was told that at the trial of a Fingallian for stealing a cow, the Mayor told the prisoner, he was sure he was a rascal for he saw a rogue in his face, which the Irishman answered, My soul good me Lord Mayor, ee never knew me face was a looking glass before.

They have also a Recorder, who at present is one Mr. Handcock who besides the reputation that he has for his knowledge of the laws has also acquired that of a bold and just magistrate, severely putting the law in execution against lewd and wicked people, without regard to any degree of quality or riches. Instances of which are frequently seen in his punishing swearers with [2]o shillings for each oath according to a new Act of Parliament, and setting insolvent persons in the stocks. And many of the strolling courteous ladies of the town have by his orders been forced to expose their lily white skin down to the waist at a cart's tail, by which he is become at once the fear and hatred of the lewd, and love and satisfaction of sober persons .

The Mayor is elected by the Aldermen who commonly go by seniority on [blank] and within ten days the election is to be noted to the government else it is void, and on the day after Michaelmas day he is sworn before the barons of the Exchequer, as also are the Sheriffs. Every third year all the Company mounted in troops under their Masters as Captains ride with the sword round all the franchises of the city. This day the Mayor is general of the field, and a man rides into the sea as far as his horse will carry him and hurls a dart as far as he can, and so far the city liberties extend that way.

Among one of their by-laws which prescribes the manner of riding the franchises, or fringes (as they call them), they are strictly forbidden to ride with soogaans, that is stirrups made with thumb-ropes of hay or straw, as many of the Irish do to this day.

Another custom they had, which has been but very lately abolished, to march to a place called Cullenswood within two miles of the city, in very formal array, on a day they called Black Monday, where their wives and friends follow after and with junkets and good things solace one the other. Now the reason of this was, because that before the utter reduction of the Irish the part of the country called the county of Wicklow, towards which Cullenswood lies, was then possessed by the Byrnes, Tooles and Kavanaghs, three Irish septs, now the English of Dublin were so secure that one Easter Monday they with their friends went to this wood to be merry under the green bushes, but the Irish surprised them and slew above three hundred in the midst of their jollity, ever since when they have gone to that same wood one Monday yearly to provoke those dastardly murdering Irish to come and play the like trick again if they dare, though there are but few of that breed left.

Every Sunday in the forenoon the Lord Mayor and Aldermen, sheriffs and some one of the Companies on foot in their gowns salute the government on the Tholsel stairs as it passes by, and then attend it to church. The arms of the city are Azure three castles argent.

I am informed the Lord Mayor's revenue is £500 out of the exchequer and the city gives him so much yearly besides other perquisites. In High Street which stands at one corner of the Tholsel on Saturdays and Wednesdays is held a market where friezes and linen cloth are sold by the country people, in such throngs that you can hardly pass among them without danger of being lousy. At the upper end of this street stands a place called Cornmarket, which formerly was such, but that market is removed because of the narrowness of it, into St. Thomas Street in the western suburb without Newgate, which is the prison for malefactors. The next place I strolled to was the Cathedral of Saint Patrick's reckoned one of the oldest churches now standing in this kingdom. It is a very lofty building with three aisles, the middlemost one is a noble one; the Archbishop has his throne in the Cathedral, which has a very stately organ that they say cost £900. Near the altar is a monument erected at the burial place of the earl of Cork; under the roof of this pile is the parish church also, and another large one to which the French refugees resort to divine worship, they say when this church was built the workmen were hired at a penny per day, so cheap were victuals here, and so scarce was money, but I incline to believe the former, because they say a cow should be grazed for a whole year for a pound of butter in days of yore. To this cathedral belong a dean, chancellor, chanter and 22 prebends, for all whom there are respectively stalls. The choristers that serve here serve also in Christchurch, and some certain day in every term they go into the court of Exchequer when the judges are sitting and read prayers and sing an anthem. The University in their caps and gowns attend the Provost who is preceded by his mace to St. Patrick's church every Sunday in the afternoon in Lent, where one of the senior fellows take their turn to preach, and on Wednesdays in Lent the Lord Lieutenant goes thither to church. It stands on one of the lowest grounds about the town, yet its steeple is higher than [that] of any other church. I saw a funeral here, and the corpse was buried in water, which they say springs up here upon making any ordinary grave. From hence I straggled to Sepulchres, where the Archbishop's Palace stands, it is an old building and little remarkable is in it besides his Grace, who is allowed by all men to be a man of great learning, he is lord of the manor of Sepulchres, holds courts for deciding of differences by a seneschal, he has a marshal and prison for debtors. After I had visited the other churches that are eleven in all, only that which lies on the north side of the river and called St. Michan's, is by Act of Parliament now divided into three parishes, and they are building two new churches there ; I say after I had paid my devotions to these religious houses, I took a turn to the Playhouse, a place very contrary to its owners for they on their outsides make the best show, having very little within, whilst it is very ordinary in its outward appearance, but looks much better on the inside, with its stage, pit, boxes, two galleries, lattices and music loft, though I must confess that even these like other false beauties receive a lustre from their lamps and candles. It stands in a dirty street called Smock Alley, which I think is no unfit name for a place where such great opportunities are given for making smock bargains. Hither I came in my best clothes and powdered wig, not like a bookseller but a beau, though not so much to be seen as to see new faces and new follies. However the theatre be applauded by a modern gentleman for the representation of those things which so mightily promote virtue, religion, and monarchical government, for my part I thought vice which fundamentally destroys all those things is here as well as in other theatres so charmingly discovered, as to make men rather love than abhor it like the judge who on the bench discovering the arts of some cow-stealers to disguise the beasts by altering the figure of their horns, taught a poor fellow the trick, who putting it in practice was brought to the gallows. However to give the devil his due there are some actors here no way inferior to those in London, nor are the spectators by what I saw one degree less in vanity and foppery than those in another place.

Since his grace the duke of Ormond went to Kilkenny the players with all their appurtenances strolled thither, to entertain the company there as they gave out, though everyone knows where the carrion is the crows will follow, for Dublin was then without much of the people that are usually in it, many of them in the summer retiring into the country.

The next thing I am to give an account of is my perambulation to the liberties of Donore and Thomas Court Manors belonging to the earl of Meath; this suburb lies to the south part of the city and is a large and spacious one able to furnish out some thousands of brawny weavers and other tradesmen of good reputation and substance, for the greatest part of the woollen trade wrought in Dublin is here, and a large handsome street called the Coom has little in it more than clothiers shops and weavers' houses. I am informed that there are not four papists masters of families dwelling in all this liberty, so little is that noble lord an encourager of those people.

Another of my inquisitive rambles is to the castle, the place of residence for the chief governor. It is encompassed with a wall and dry ditch over which is a drawbridge and within that an iron gate, opposite to which in the inner court are two brass field pieces planted, as also some others on top of one of the towers, and yet it is no place of great strength, I mean such as is able to endure the battery of great guns, though it can command all the city from its towers. It has an handsome guardhouse for the soldiers and other rooms for the officers, for a foot company with three commissioned officers daily mount the guard, and whenever the government go out or come in they are received with colours flying and drums beating as the King is at Whitehall, and indeed the grandeur they live in here is not much inferior to what you see in London if you make allowances for the number of great men at court there. The building is handsome without much magnificence on the outside, you enter the house up a noble stairs and find several stately rooms one of which is called the Presence chamber and has a chair of state with a canopy over it. One part of the house stands over a large stone gallery supported by several pillars of stone. (Here describe lord Galway's apartment).[4]

At the back of the house lies a broad terrace walk the length of the building the walls covered with greens and flower pots, from hence on a stone arch over a little river you descend by two spacious pair of stone stairs into the garden, which is handsomely laid out into grass plots with green and gravel walks, and at the north side there are two rows of flourishing lime-trees, beneath which lies another grass walk. This garden was made by that great man the Lord Sidney, now earl of Romney, when he was chief governor.

To the castle belongs an officer called the Constable of the Castle, who receives prisoners of state when committed, as the Lieutenant of the Tower does. To the north side lies the chapel to which the lord Galway goes constantly every morning to prayers, and at his return spends sometime in receiving petitions, which he answers with all the sweetness and readiness that any petitioner can wish for in so great a man.

Next the chapel is the office of the Ordinance, near which the King's gunsmiths and armourers work, before these buildings lies a large piece of ground called the Stable-yard, on one side of which are the King's stables, which as they are not extraordinary so they are no way despicable, but convenient and big enough ; in this yard two companies of foot parade every morning, one of which mounts the town guard and the other that of the Castle. The little river which I now mentioned runs here, on the other side of which stands the coach-houses, and biggest hay-stacks that ever I saw.

[4] These words appear in the MS. but apparently Dunton did not carry out his intention in this respect.

After I had done gazing at court I went to view the Council Chamber in Essex Street, where the Lords Justices were at Council, and it happening to be a public day poor Peelgarlick had admittance as readily as my lord. It is a large house to which you ascend by an handsome pair of wooden steps. The Council Chamber is a very spacious room with a table at which more than forty may sit, at the upper end stand chairs for the Lords Justices, at lower end of the table a rail goes across the room, which serves as a bar when there is any public pleading before them. . . . .

Opposite to this is the Custom house, where the Commissioners of the Revenue sit, they are [blank] in number and manage the whole Revenue of the nation.

Here is an handsome Quay where all the goods as well exported as imported, are brought and entered in the Customhouse books, and all such that are not so entered are forfeited to the King if discovered. I was told of a clergyman in this town, that coming from England brought some silk to make his wife a manto and petticoat, that to avoid paying custom he had wrapped it about his body under his canonical coat, but the tide waiters discovered it, and by his parsimony he lost his sheep[5] for a pennorth of tar, and the Sunday after, he was observed to preach on this text, Render to Caesar the things that are Caesar's etc. Here are storehouses to lodge the goods in until their duty be paid, and a large crane with a wheel in which a man walks to turn it (as dogs do in the wheel of a jack) for housing goods out of the gabbards which bring them up from the ships, there lies abundance of wool on the Quay to be exported, and a great deal of French wines that are here landed. A Quaker called [blank] imported a great parcel of white and red wines which lay on the custom-house quay for some time, which with some other goods are every night watched by some officers of the Customs in a little house appointed for that purpose; but the Quaker used to come every night with a small boat and hogsheads in it, and drew the wine out of the vessels that lay there and carried it away, and filled the vessels with water so that when they were all emptied he came to pay the custom for them but upon search they were found to contain nothing but water;

[5] In the modern version of the phrase, " to spoil the ship for a ha'porth of tar " the word " ship " is said to be a corruption of " sheep ".

the man made a great splutter about the loss of his wine, the Commissioners were at a stand and knew not what to do, for the trick could not be proved upon anyone, and so the King lost his money, upon which one said that Christ the divine turned water into wine [*blank*] the Quaker turned wine into water.

On this river called the Liffey stands six bridges belonging to Dublin, that next the custom-house is called Essex Bridge because begun when Arthur earl of Essex was Lord Lieutenant; the next is called Ormond Bridge, next to that stands the old bridge, westward of this is the New Bridge, then Bloody Bridge, so called because the city mob attempted to pull it down, and in dispersing them several were killed; west of this is Island Bridge near the soldiers' hospital by and by. Most of these divide the city from the northern suburbs, which by itself makes a large town almost as big as Southwark containing now three parishes, though until this present session of Parliament it was but one, when 'twas divided into three by an act, the then minister of it Dr. Pooley being made bishop of Cloyne; the only things remarkable in it are the Inns, and bowling-green, and an hospital for about 60 boys who have a chaplain, and schoolmaster, they are clad in blue coats lined with yellow, and as they grow up they are put to trades. The Inns is a handsome street lying upon the river. It has a cloister in which is a large hall where the judges and other men of law dine in term time at commons. Here also is kept the Rolls office of the kingdom; the present Master of the Rolls is the Lord Berkeley; it is said to be worth £2000 per annum. The Bowling-green is the only thing that Dublin exceeds or equals London in. It is a very large piece of ground well walled in, and the walls covered with fruit-trees: the southern wall has an handsome terrace walk its whole length and, for the evenness of so large a ground it much surpasses the Green at Marrowbone, though there be not the tenth part of the money played here as there. Northwest of this is a great plot of land walled, and called the Palace Garden, 'tis a piece of ground which the city gave to James the late duke of Ormond to build upon, a wall divides it from a field called the Hospital Green where the citizens walk and refresh themselves in the open air as you do at Moorfields. Here 'tis I took up the pleasantest lodging

I had in Dublin on Archers Hill at the house of one Orson, who with his wife an ancient couple seemed to me like Adam and Eve in Paradise, he employing himself in his pretty garden and she within doors in making milk-water, of which she distils very large quantities. I think myself obliged to let them live as long as this paper holds in gratitude for the tendernesses they shewed me. Hereabouts are very noble piles, houses that yield at this day an hundred pounds a year rent.

Not far from this pleasant lodging stands the hospital of Kilmainham, built by Charles the 2nd for poor soldiers on an high ground on the south side of the river. It is a noble building and looks [more] like a palace than what it is, with four spacious fronts ; the inner part of the building is supported by pillars of stone, and has four great piazzas flagged with broad stone, it bears as great an air of grandeur as that at Chelsea ; within is a large square court. Over these piazzas are galleries equal to them, into which the doors of the chambers open. It is so large that after the battle of Aughrim there were 1200 sick and wounded men in it, but then the hall and galleries had beds laid in them. The hall is spacious and suitable to the house, and has a clock in the middle of the ceiling. Here the soldiers at the ring of the bell come to their meals, and are well served with wholesome and cleanly food.[6] At the east end of the hall a door opens into the chapel, with pews and galleries, the carved work about the altar is esteemed the best in Ireland and not inferior to any in England and indeed to me it appeared very fine.

To this Hospital there is a Governor who is the Earl of Meath, a deputy Governor one Major Stroud, a chaplain, a physician and surgeon and apothecary. The place of governor is said to be £500 per annum, and indeed I saw nothing wanting here for the comfortable subsistence in their latter days for those who have undergone the fatigues of a soldier's life. Without the wall nearer to the river stands the Infirmary in which also the steward of the hospital and his family dwell. The present chaplain is a person of a fair character, one who in the late wars was minister of Mullingar,

---

[6] Many interesting details of the life of the inmates and officials of this institution about the time Dunton visited it are given in *The Story of the Royal Hospital, Kilmainham* (Childers and Stewart) 1921 edn. See particularly Appendix VIII of that work.

and black haired, he was snapped some way by the Irish and scurvily used by them, so far as to threaten him with gelding, which put the poor gentleman into such a fright as in one night (I am told) changed many of his black hairs into grey, which makes him at this day look hoary. To the south side of this hospital stands Kilmainham where formerly was a convent of friars, but no marks of it are now to be seen, though one of its priors carried to King Henry to the siege of Boulogne (as I remember) 1500 men. In this town stands the jail and session house of the county of Dublin, with one of the same family of the three legged gentleman at Tyburn to give malefactors their exit out of this world. Here is a large ground plot called in for manufactory, but that is at a stand as they say by reason that England is so much disgusted at the great progress they make in working up wool.